Are Mormons Christians?

Are Mormons Christians

STEPHEN E. ROBINSON

Bookcraft
Salt Lake City, Utah

For Janet—the truest Christian I know

Library of Congress Catalog Card Number: 90–86351

ISBN 0–88494–784–X

5th Printing, 1996

Printed in the United States of America

Contents

Contents

Preface

In July 1986 a group of evangelical Christians and former Mormons held a news conference in Salt Lake City and subsequently presented a petition to The Church of Jesus Christ of Latter-day Saints demanding that it stop referring to itself as a "Christian" church. The petition had been signed by 20,543 individuals from 49 states and 31 foreign countries.[1]

The reaction to this petition in Utah was largely one of consternation. After all, the Saints asked themselves, is not the name of our church The Church of *Jesus Christ* of Latter-day Saints? Do we not worship Christ? Is not the Book of Mormon another testament of Jesus Christ? The Utah Saints shook their heads and wondered how it was possible that anyone could seriously doubt that the Latter-day Saints were Christians. For several weeks afterward letters to the editors of the major Utah newspapers clearly indicated that the petition had stirred strong feelings on both sides of the question. Attacks and defenses, devotions and vituperations were all displayed in the controversy, but there is little evidence that either side really understood the basic issues involved.

The charge that Mormons are not Christians may nonplus the Saints on Utah's Wasatch Front—who seldom hear it or, when they do, simply dismiss it as too silly to be taken seriously —but in those areas where Latter-day Saints are a minority of the population, this is often the most commonly heard criticism of the LDS church and its doctrines. For the most part, even these

Latter-day Saints find the charge incomprehensible; and without comprehension it is very difficult to offer a coherent response.

It is hoped that this book will be of service on two fronts —that it will make the accusation that Latter-day Saints aren't Christians comprehensible to the Latter-day Saints, and that it will also help them in forming an intelligent and informed response to that accusation. This book is not meant, however, to provide ammunition for those contentious souls who simply want to carry on a war of words with the anti-Mormons, for the spirit of contention is always un-Christian (see D&C 10:63).

It is not my purpose in these pages to prove, or even to argue, that the LDS church is true or that its doctrines are correct, even though I believe both of those propositions. Rather, I will attempt to show why the arguments used to exclude Latter-day Saints from the "Christian" world are flawed. The operating principle behind most of my arguments will not be rectitude but equity—what is sauce for the goose is sauce for the gander. That is, if Augustine or Luther or John Paul II can express opinions or insist on beliefs that differ from the Christian mainstream and yet still be considered Christians, then Joseph Smith and Brigham Young cannot be disqualified from bearing that title when they express the same or similar opinions. If theological or ecclesiastical diversity can be tolerated among mainstream Christian churches without charges of their being "non-Christian," then diversity of a similar kind, or to a similar degree, ought to be tolerated in the Latter-day Saints. This is simply an issue of playing on a level field.

At one time Protestant and Catholic denominations did make charges against each other, each claiming that the other (or others) was not Christian. But in the almost five hundred years since the Reformation, Protestants and Catholics have become used to each other and, with the exception of certain fundamentalist groups, are willing to tolerate the differences between themselves. They see these differences as being "all in the family," and refer to each other as "Christians" in a generic sense, though they may still disagree with each other's doctrines.

The problem is that the Latter-day Saints have only been around for 160 years, and the more senior denominations have not yet become used to us, nor do they yet extend to us the courtesies and the toleration they now automatically extend to each other. I will maintain in the following pages that the Latter-day Saints are often the victims of a theological double standard, being labelled "non-Christian" for opinions and practices that are freely tolerated in other mainstream denominations. Where this is the case, I must insist that the charges are not only unfair but are logically defective. For if person A holds an opinion with which other Christians disagree, and yet person A remains a Christian in the common estimation, then person B may not logically be declared to be non-Christian for holding the same opinion—what is sauce for the goose is sauce for the gander. No honest Christian, Mormon or non-Mormon, should be satisfied with results arrived at with the aid of an unlevel playing field or a theological double standard.

Many complex and even contradictory arguments are offered by those who would exclude the Latter-day Saints from the family of "Christian" churches. These arguments generally fall into one of six basic categories: (1) exclusion by definition; (2) exclusion by misrepresentation; (3) exclusion by name-calling (the ad hominem exclusion); (4) the historical or traditional exclusion; (5) the canonical or biblical exclusion; and (6) the doctrinal exclusion. In each of these broad categories there are certain subtle assumptions about the nature, history, and doctrine of the Christian religion that must be defined and examined before the exclusions based on them can be considered. I find that, upon close examination, these assumptions and/or the arguments based on them turn out to be either illogical or unfair.

The reader should note that where I have used examples and illustrations from antiquity, these are taken only from what are commonly considered orthodox Christian sources and not from Gnostic, Marcionite, Manichaean, or other heterodox writings. Also, in referring to modern authorities I have cited only mainline non-LDS scholars whose work is widely known and respected, usually the consensus experts in their fields. The reader will find that there has been no stacking the deck with eccentric "authorities" either ancient or modern.

In the following chapters I shall use the terms *orthodox* and *orthodoxy* to refer to traditional, mainstream Christianity. This is merely for convenience and does not indicate that I accept "orthodox" Christianity as theologically correct, or that I accept any implication that Latter-day Saints are in the strict sense "*un*orthodox."

Finally, it should be understood that I do not speak officially for the LDS church or for Brigham Young University. While I believe the opinions expressed here to be soundly based, I alone am responsible for them.

1

The Exclusion by Definition

What is a Christian? The term is found three times in the New Testament (Acts 11:26; 26:28; 1 Peter 4:16), but it is not defined in any of these passages. According to *Webster's Third New International Dictionary* the term *Christian* may be defined in a number of ways, but the most common is "one who believes or professes or is assumed to believe in Jesus Christ and the truth as taught by him: an adherent of Christianity: one who has accepted the Christian religious and moral principles of life: one who has faith in and has pledged allegiance to God thought of as revealed in Christ: one whose life is conformed to the doctrines of Christ." The second most common meaning is "a member of a church or group professing Christian doctrine or belief."

Under either of these two most common definitions in the English language, Latter-day Saints qualify as Christians. Moreover, these are the definitions that most Latter-day Saints themselves would use in applying the term *Christian* to other denominations. Thus, even though Latter-day Saints feel very strongly that theirs is the true Church of Jesus Christ, they still accept Protestants and Catholics in all their varieties as Christians because these denominations believe in Jesus as the Christ and attempt to follow his teachings, however differently they may interpret them. While it is true that there are doctrinal differences, sometimes serious, between Christian denominations, it is generally accepted that each follows Christ as it best understands him. As the dictionary indicates, this is the way that most people use the term *Christian*, as a generic noun that tolerates doctrinal differences and denominational variations among those who believe Jesus Christ to be the Son of God and the Savior of the world. If one understands the term *Christian* in this way, then the charge that Mormons* are not Christians is a serious charge indeed.

Nonstandard Definitions

Most of the time, however, those who make this charge are not using the term *Christian* with this definition in mind at all. He who defines a term controls a term. For example, if the Latter-day Saints defined the term *Christian* to mean "one who believes in the divine calling of the Prophet Joseph Smith and in the inspired nature of the Book of Mormon," then they would be *technically* correct (based on their own private definition of the term) in concluding that only Latter-day Saints are Christians. It is unlikely, however, that the rest of the world would agree with such a parochial and distorted definition, and Latter-day Saints would likely (and rightly) be accused of trying to stack the deck through the manipulation of language. For Mormons to define *Christians* as "people who believe what Mormons believe" and then conclude that non-Mormons aren't Christians would be nothing more than to say that non-Mormons aren't Mormons —without any consideration for what they may or may not believe about Jesus.

In fact, this manipulating of terms is exactly what some do in excluding the Latter-day Saints from consideration as Christians. They define *Christian* not in the generic sense of common usage, but in a narrow sectarian sense that excludes anyone whose doctrine differs from their own. Individuals who wouldn't tolerate a denominationally exclusive definition of the term *Christian* if it excluded them will often accept such a tactic if the tables are turned and the trick is played on someone else. Thus on the surface these individuals seem to be making the very serious charge that the Latter-day Saints do not believe in Jesus Christ or do not

---

* Both here and in the pages that follow I shall occasionally use the popular term *Mormon* for the sake of clarity, for nuance, or for proper context, even though the correct term is *Latter-day Saint*.

attempt to follow his teachings, but in reality they are only saying that the Latter-day Saints understand Jesus Christ differently and worship him differently than they do.

Any way you look at it, this game is rigged. If you define a Christian as one who believes in the fundamentals of conservative Protestantism, for example, then only fundamentalist Protestants will be Christians. If you define a Christian as one who accepts the leadership and authority of Pope John Paul II, then only Roman Catholics will be Christians. If you define a Christian as one who accepts the authority of Archbishop Makarios or of Pope Shenouda, then only the Greek or Coptic Orthodox, respectively, can be Christians. Playing this kind of word game is like defining a duck as an aquatic bird with a broad, flat bill, short legs, webbed feet, and brown feathers, and then arguing that female mallards are ducks but males are not because the latter's feathers are the wrong color.

Of course there certainly are those who define *Christian* denominationally in just this way in order to exclude Latter-day Saints and anyone else whose feathers are the wrong color, just as there are those who define *human being* as necessarily meaning "male," or "Caucasian," or "Anglo-Saxon." There is usually little that can be done to get such individuals to change their definition to include the whole class and not just those with "the right colored feathers," but we *can* point out to them the logical fallacy of using nonstandard definitions or an overly specific taxonomy for exclusionary purposes.

It is ironic that one version of the exclusion by definition tactic was used against ancient Christians by pagan opponents who, according to Wayne A. Meeks, "often denounced the new cult as 'a superstition' and its members as 'atheists.' "[1] No matter how much Christians protested the unfairness of this charge, insisting that they worshipped God, their persecutors countered that Christians did not worship *the* gods — that is, the right *sort* of gods, the *pagan* gods — and were therefore "atheists." With this specialized definition of *atheist*, all the charge really meant was that Christians worshipped God differently than pagans, but the slander gave the impression to the masses — as it was designed to — that the Christians were godless and irreligious. Of course this made hating and persecuting the Christians much easier and made it much more difficult for the Christians to get a fair hearing. This same tactic is now being used against the Latter-day Saints by other Christians who don't like the way we worship Christ and would therefore deny us the title of Christian.

Excluding More Than the Latter-day Saints

If the term *Christian* is understood to mean someone who believes that Jesus is the Christ, the Son of God and the Savior of the world, and who believes that the Old and New Testaments contain his teachings, then the Mormons are Christians. It is simply a matter of historical record that the Latter-day Saints affirm all these propositions. Although the Latter-day Saints may differ in details of doctrinal interpretation (that is, have different colored feathers from other kinds of Christians), they certainly share the basic taxonomic similarities of the class.

On the other hand, if the term *Christian* is defined in a sectarian way to mean "those who believe as we do," then the sect in question might be able to say Mormons aren't Christians (using the term in their private, nonstandard sense), but all this statement really means is that Mormons aren't Baptists, or Pentecostals, or whatever—and we already knew that. The charge in this case is certainly not as serious as it would be if the excluders used the common definitions. But their use of customized definitions makes their charge against the Mormons not only trivial but useless. It certainly has no bearing on whether Latter-day Saints believe in Jesus Christ.

What the average "Christian" (used here in the inclusive sense) reader needs to bear in mind, regardless of his or her own denomination, is that those who exclude by definition usually exclude considerably more people than just the Latter-day Saints. If one allows the term *Christian* to be defined in a nonstandard way to mean evangelical Protestantism, for example, then Mormons are indeed excluded, but so are Roman Catholics, Greek Orthodox, and most other kinds of Protestants—any duck whose feathers are not exactly the right color. Even among the most conservative Protestants this same exclusion has recently been used to declare as "heretics" and non-Christians such evangelists as Pat Robertson, Robert Schuller, and Oral Roberts—anyone at all who disagrees with the narrow sectarian view. For those who employ this exclusion, the "family of Christian churches" is usually very small indeed. Their operating definition of a Christian is "a member of the *true* church [*my* church]," or "one who believes what I believe." Not even the Latter-day Saints, who feel very strongly that theirs is the true Church, would define being a Christian in such a limited way.

On one occasion, when I was in the East lecturing on this topic to a group of ministers from various denominations, one person in particular kept insisting that Mormons were not Christians and that for this reason everything I had said was invalid. So I asked him—with Roman Catholic parish priests in the audience—if Roman Catholics were Christians in his understanding. He replied that they could be, but that they usually weren't, because they believed in salvation through the sacraments of the Catholic church and not through a ''being saved'' experience alone. I asked him again—with a Greek Orthodox priest present in the audience—if the Eastern Orthodox were Christians. He answered, ''Only if they believe what Christians [that is, *his* kind of Christians] believe.'' Then I asked him if liberal Protestants who do not accept the fundamentalist Christian theology were Christians. ''Absolutely not,'' was the reply. ''They are traitors to the cause of Christ.''

While many of the ministers present at that meeting would have agreed originally with this man's statement that Mormons were not Christians, they quickly became incensed when the same charge, *on the same grounds and for the same reasons*, was levelled against them. In fact, all this particular individual was saying is that Mormons, Catholics, Orthodox, and liberal Protestants alike are not Christian fundamentalists. The hidden premise in his argument was that if one did not believe what he believed, then one was not a Christian. But surely if this hidden premise and the reasoning based upon it are to be rejected when applied to other Christian denominations, then they must be rejected when applied to the Latter-day Saints as well.

Fundamentalists and other sectarians are free, I suppose, to define the word *Christian* any way they want to for their own purposes. They can define themselves as the only genuine Christians in the whole world and then shut *everybody* else out, as long as the rest of Christendom understands that that is how they are using the language, and that coming from them the assertion that ''Mormons aren't Christians'' simply means ''Mormons disagree with us.''

Christianity by Consensus

Now, it could be argued that the term *non-Christian* should be applied to anything not found, taught, or believed within the family of Christian churches, but this assertion meets with certain difficulties. First of all, it begs the question. Shall the Latter-day Saints be considered as part of the family of Christian churches that might be surveyed to determine what is "Christian"? Whether one says yea or nay, one must assume in advance the results of the survey. Begging the question is assuming in advance the results of the proposition supposedly being tested—the proposition being, in this case, "Are Latter-day Saints Christians?"

Second, the New Testament tells us that Paul most assuredly knew things, believed things that could not be shared with some Christians (see 1 Corinthians 3:1–2) or with any other Christians at all (2 Corinthians 12:2–4). Did his knowing and believing things not taught in the Bible, things unknown to other Christians, render Paul a "non-Christian"? Surely not. This specialized definition of *Christian* simply doesn't work.

The New Testament itself does not present a very narrow view of who was a disciple and who was not. In Acts 18:24–28 we read about Apollos, who was "instructed in the way of the Lord" but incompletely. Eloquent as Apollos was, his doctrine was defective until Aquila and Priscilla "expounded unto him the way of God more perfectly." Yet there is no indication that he was not considered a Christian before he was set straight. Similarly, Paul found "certain disciples" near Ephesus who were so imperfectly taught that it was decided to baptize them over again (Acts 19:1–7). Nevertheless, imperfect as their understanding was originally, they, like Apollos, were called disciples, even though certainly there was room on their part for doctrinal improvement. The Christians at Corinth were so immature that Paul couldn't teach them the meat (the heavy doctrines) of the gospel at all; nevertheless Paul still addressed them as Saints (1 Corinthians 3:2; 1:2).

The letters of Paul make it absolutely clear that the law of Moses is fulfilled in the gospel of Christ and is no longer binding as a requirement for salvation. Thus most would consider this a "Christian" doctrine. Yet in Acts 21:20 we read that James said to Paul, "Thou seest, brother, how many thousands of Jews there are which believe; and they are all zealous of the law." These believers were not thrown out of the Church, even though they did not yet understand the fundamental doctrine of how the law was fulfilled in Christ. On the contrary, James even suggested to Paul a public relations maneuver designed to soothe their Jewish-Christian sensibilities (Acts 21:23–24). Even though their doctrine was defective, they were still counted as "believers" and tolerated, even coddled, in the Jerusalem Church. Now, if Paul, the champion of grace, could put himself to great trouble for the sake of Jewish Christians whose doctrine was, in part, in conflict with his own, should not modern Christians of all denominations who disagree with each other be cautious about labelling those with doctrinal differences as entirely "non-Christian"?

Summary

In summary, most of the time the charge that Latter-day Saints are not Christians has absolutely nothing to do with LDS belief or nonbelief in Jesus Christ, or with LDS acceptance or rejection of the New Testament as the word of God. If the term *Christian* is used, as it is in standard English, to mean someone who accepts Jesus Christ as the Son of God and the Savior of the world, then the charge that Mormons aren't Christians is false. However, if the word *Christian* is used in a sectarian sense to mean belief in Christ or in the New Testament according to a particular denominational view, then the charge is trivial and uninformative; it is merely another way of saying Latter-day Saints don't agree with the denomination making the charge. Typically those who define *Christian* in this latter sense exclude not only Mormons but also any individual who may disagree with them, whether that individual puts his faith in Jesus Christ or not. All but the narrowest ideologues ought to be able to detect the logical fallacies involved in the exclusion by definition.

2

The Exclusion
by Misrepresentation

Simply put, the exclusion by misrepresentation is the attempt to condemn Latter-day Saints for things they *don't* believe. One of the fundamental liberties guaranteed under the Constitution of the United States is that people can believe and worship as they choose. No group or individual has the right to force their doctrine on anyone else. As a corollary to this, most would agree that it is also the right of any church or religion to define and interpret its own doctrines for its own use. The Methodists decide what Methodists believe, and the Baptists decide what Baptists believe; thus the doctrines of Methodism will be what Methodists determine they are and not what someone else says they are or must be.

Anti-Mormon Mind Readers

Yet time and again the Latter-day Saints are denied this basic privilege of defining and interpreting their own doctrines. Quite frequently a Latter-day Saint attempting to explain the tenets of his or her faith to non-Mormons will be interrupted by some self-styled expert who says, "No, that's *not* what you believe; *this* is what you believe!" There generally follows a recital of some hocus-pocus that is certainly not taught by the LDS church. Ponder the absurdity of it — "*You* don't know what you believe, but *I* know what you believe; I know your thoughts better than you do!''

Many times in my professional career I have had occasion to say, ''I'm sorry, but I don't believe that,'' only to be assured most forcefully by some antagonist that really, privately, secretly, I did *too* believe it. ''Take my word for it,'' I have responded, ''*I* am the world's authority on what *I* believe—and I have *never* believed what you say I do!'' Usually such a declaration on my part is to no avail, for these individuals have already decided in their own minds what my personal beliefs and the beliefs of the LDS church are, and they will not generally accept any testimony to the contrary. Thus I am denied the right to define my own beliefs.

Such individuals usually insist that Mormon doctrine is better understood and more authoritatively interpreted by non-Mormons than by Mormons. With a reasonably knowledgeable Latter-day Saint right in front of them saying, ''That is not and never has been my belief or the doctrine of my church,'' they prefer to believe some anti-Mormon pamphlet or cleric. In fact it has frequently become an article of *their* faith to insist that Latter-day Saints believe absurd and silly things that no Latter-day Saint in the world has ever heard taught as doctrine. Shall Mormon doctrine be what the Mormons say it is or what their opponents say it is?

When non-Mormons attempt to impose doctrines on the Latter-day Saints or interpret them for us, the resulting fictions generally fall into one of three categories: outright fabrications, distortions of genuine LDS doctrines into unrecognizable forms, or the representation of anomalies within the LDS tradition as mainline or official LDS teaching.

Fabrication

A little background on the issue of outright fabrication is provided by an experience of the Procter and Gamble Company. Somewhere on the extreme fringes of the religious right the rumor was started in the early 1980s that Procter and Gamble, the soap company, was owned by satanists and that all of P&G's profits went to the Church of Satan. Apparently some ''Christian'' had noticed the venerable P&G trademark, which shows the man in the moon and thirteen stars honoring the thirteen colonies, and in the total absence of any evidence decided that this was a satanic symbol. Soon photocopied sheets detailing the sins of P&G were circulating in every part of the country, and as the story spread, it grew. Ultimately it was claimed that P&G was wholly owned by the satanic church and that its officials had appeared on the Donahue show discussing their links to satanism.

Finding themselves attacked by religious fanatics, Procter and Gamble fought back. Expecting that any story so absurd and so easily disproved could be quickly stopped, the company established a toll-free public information number and hired private detectives to find out who was spreading the lies. In many states lawsuits were filed against those circulating literature containing the false stories. Sent to all ministers in affected areas were public relations packets with statements from Billy Graham, Jerry Falwell, Jimmy Draper of the Southern Baptist Convention, and Joseph Bernardin, the Roman Catholic archbishop of Cincinnati, all certifying that the story was a lie. Statements from the Donahue people denied that anyone from P&G had ever even been on that program, or that Donahue had ever even done a show on a related topic.

All to no avail—the religious extremists whom P&G was up against believed and printed whatever they wanted to, regardless of the quality or quantity of the contradictory evidence. Having the truth was nowhere near as important to them as having a target. After trying for years with all the legal, financial, and public relations resources of one of America's largest companies, an incredulous P&G finally had to throw in the towel and get rid of its trademark. They simply could not stop the willful and intentional fabrications of religious extremists.

The point is this: If an entity as innocuous as a soap company can become the target of religious irrationality and be totally unable to stop the subsequent campaign of lies, what chance do the Latter-day Saints have? For it is basically the same element that ambushed Procter and Gamble that produces and circulates the most outrageous fabrications about the Latter-day Saints and their beliefs. But the Latter-day Saints don't hire lawyers and private detectives; there are no mass mailings or public relations campaigns to counter the fabrications. The Latter-day Saints just continue to teach their beliefs, their *real* beliefs, to those who will listen. Unfortunately, even people who are too knowledgeable to have fallen for the Procter and Gamble stuff are sometimes taken in by the same kind of outrageous literature if it is written against the Latter-day Saints.

One day in 1983, when our family was living in Pennsylvania, our daughter Sarah, then ten years old, came home from school visibly upset. The subject of the Mormon pioneers had come up in class, and the teacher had asked if anyone knew anything about the Mormons. Before Sarah could respond, one of her classmates said, "My daddy says Mormons are people who live in Utah and worship idols." Sarah quickly answered back, "Well, I'm a Mormon, and we don't worship idols." But the teacher would not back her up, and many of her classmates never did believe her, largely because they had already been taught in their Sunday schools that Mormons do worship idols or Joseph Smith. Once again the first-person testimony of a live Latter-day Saint was rejected in favor of a popular anti-Mormon fabrication.

This state of affairs reminds one of the popular Christian notions of Jewish belief that circulated during the Middle Ages (and later). No matter what Jews said to the contrary, no matter what the evidence indicated, many Christians insisted that Jews secretly practiced the ritual mutilation and murder of Christian children. Over the centuries thousands of Jews have been killed as a result of this and other Christian fabrications. This Christian view of what Jews believed and practiced had become part of popular Christian faith, even though it had nothing to do with the actual beliefs and practices of Judaism.[1]

Distortion

A close relative of the exclusion by fabrication is the exclusion by distortion. The only difference is that distortions are not entirely groundless, like fabrications, but are related to doctrines that the Latter-day Saints actually do believe. Yet the same objections hold for the exclusion by distortion as for the exclusion by fabrication. Latter-day Saints can't reasonably or logically be declared non-Christian for beliefs they do not hold, even if the distortion is *similar* to actual LDS beliefs.

Let Them Speak for Themselves

When I was just out of graduate school, I was assigned to teach a class outside my usual area of expertise called Roman Catholic Thought. My colleagues stated at the time that nothing could be more ecumenical than a Mormon teaching Roman Catholic thought at a Methodist college, and indeed it turned out to be one of the most rewarding experiences of my career. After many years of hearing mostly non-Catholics explain Catholicism to me, I actually read *Catholic* theologians explaining their *own* beliefs. I learned that Catholicism was not the religion I had been led to believe it was. For the class I assigned and used only books that were marked "nihil obstat" and "imprimatur," that is, officially approved by the Catholic church. Day after day I learned along with my students and gave up distortions and misrepresentations that I had once ignorantly accepted as a part of Catholicism. The experience strengthened my already firm conviction that any religion must be allowed to speak for itself and interpret its own doctrines, and it must allow the same privilege to all others.[2]

It would seem only fair that any criticism of the Latter-day Saints must address doctrines that are actually held by them rather than doctrines merely attributed to them or interpreted for them by hostile critics. If Latter-day Saints believed that Jesus was not the Son of God but just an ordinary man, or if they worshipped someone else instead, they would be considered non-Christians — but first it would have to be established that Mormons really held such beliefs, and not merely that such beliefs were attributed to them by their enemies. Surely any reasonable investigator must grant that Latter-day Saints cannot rationally or logically be declared non-Christians on the basis of doctrines they do *not* believe.

What Is Official Doctrine?

So what constitutes genuine Mormon doctrine? What is the LDS equivalent of "nihil obstat" and "imprimatur"? What *do* the Latter-day Saints believe? Can something be said to be "Mormon" doctrine if any Latter-day Saint anywhere believes it? If my LDS grandmother believed that frogs cause warts, or that the earth is flat, does that make those ideas LDS doctrine? If some LDS missionary somewhere believes that the earth is hollow and that the lost ten tribes are hiding inside, is his or her belief therefore LDS doctrine? Of course not.

Virtually every religion has procedures for distinguishing the individual beliefs of its members from the *official* doctrines of the church, and so do the Latter-day Saints. In fact among the Mormons the procedure is remarkably similar to that of many Protestant denominations. An example of the procedure can be taken from the records of the Fiftieth Semiannual General Conference of the LDS church, 10 October 1880, when President George Q. Cannon addressed the conference:

I hold in my hand the Book of Doctrine and Covenants, and also the book, The Pearl of Great Price, which books contain revelations of God. In Kirtland, the Doctrine and Covenants in its original form, as first printed, was submitted to the officers of the Church and the members of the Church to vote upon. As there have been additions made to it by the publishing of revelations which were not contained in the original edition, it has been deemed wise to submit these books with their contents to the conference, *to see whether the conference will vote to accept the books and their contents as from God, and binding upon us as a people and as a Church.*[3]

Subsequent changes of content in the standard works of the Church have been presented similarly to the membership in general conference to receive a sustaining vote. It is that sustaining vote, by the individual members or by their representatives, that makes the changes officially binding upon the membership as the doctrine of the Church.

When Wilford Woodruff, as President of the Church, committed the Latter-day Saints to discontinue the practice of plural marriage, his official declaration was submitted to the Sixtieth Semiannual General Conference of the Church on 6 October 1890, which by unanimous vote accepted it ''as authoritative and binding.'' It was that vote which made the document *official* (it is now printed as Official Declaration — 1 in the Doctrine and Covenants). Similarly, when President Spencer W. Kimball declared in 1978, by revelation from the Lord, that the priesthood was henceforward to be given to all worthy male members, this pronouncement became Official Declaration — 2 by the sustaining vote of a general conference on 30 September 1978.

B. H. Roberts, a General Authority of the LDS church, summarized the issue perhaps as well as anyone has:

The Church has confined the sources of doctrine by which it is willing to be bound before the world to the things that God has revealed, and which the Church has officially accepted, and those alone. These would include the Bible, the Book of Mormon, the Doctrine and Covenants, the Pearl of Great Price; these have been repeatedly accepted and endorsed by the Church in general conference assembled, *and are the only sources of absolute appeal for our doctrine.*[4]

Of course it is true that many Latter-day Saints, from the Presidents of the Church and members of the Quorum of the Twelve down to individual members who may write books or articles, have expressed their own opinions on doctrinal matters. Nevertheless, until such opinions are presented to the Church in general conference and sustained by vote of the conference, they are neither binding nor the official doctrine of the Church. The critics of LDS doctrine seldom recognize this vital distinction. Rather, if any Latter-day Saint, especially one of the leading Brethren, ever said a thing, these critics take it to represent "Mormonism," regardless of the context of the particular statement and regardless of whether any other Latter-day Saint ever said it or believed it. Often the Latter-day Saints themselves are guilty of this same error and search through the *Journal of Discourses* as if it were some sort of Mormon Talmud, looking for "new" doctrines not found in the standard works and not taught in the Church today.

Usually the critics insist that the Latter-day Saints must defend as doctrine everything that Joseph Smith or Brigham Young or any other General Authority ever said. But the LDS concept of doctrine simply cannot be stretched this far. The Latter-day Saints allow that sometimes the living prophet speaks in his role as prophet and sometimes he simply states his own opinions. This distinction is no different than that made in some other Christian denominations. For example, even though Roman Catholics believe in "papal infallibility," they insist that the pope is infallible only in certain clearly defined circumstances —when he speaks *ex cathedra* on matters of faith and morals. Cannot the Latter-day Saints be allowed a similar distinction? The LDS view was expressed succinctly by Joseph Smith himself: "I told them that a prophet was a prophet only when he was acting as such."[5]

Non-Mormon critics, on the other hand, often insist that the Brethren must speak and write prophetically at *all* times. This absolutist expectation usually flows out of an extreme inerrantist view of prophecy and of scripture that is held by the critics, but not by the Latter-day Saints. The critics' belief in the Bible as absolutely perfect, without error and inspired in every word, leads them to make the same demands of anyone claiming to be a prophet. They would impose *their* inerrantist view on the Latter-day Saints and their prophets (see chapter 5 herein). But the Latter-day Saints have no such inerrantist views, neither of the scriptures nor of the prophets. The scriptures *are* the word of God, but only as far as they are translated correctly;[6] and prophets sometimes speak for the Lord, and sometimes they express their own opinions. Certainly, if the Latter-day Saints were radical inerrantists, such a view as the foregoing would be a contradiction and a scandal, but since we are not inerrantists, the view scandalizes only our inerrantist critics. B. H. Roberts expressed it in this way:

> It is not sufficient to quote sayings purported to come from Joseph Smith or Brigham Young upon matters of doctrine. Our own people also need instruction and correction in respect of this. It is common to hear some of our older brethren say, "But I heard Brother Joseph myself say so," or "Brother Brigham preached it; I heard him." But that is not the question. The question is has God said it? Was the prophet speaking officially? . . .
>
> As to the printed discourses of even leading brethren, the same principle holds. They do not constitute the court of ultimate appeal on doctrine. They may be very useful in the way of elucidation and are very generally good and sound in doctrine, but they are not the ultimate sources of the doctrines of the Church, and are not binding upon the Church. The rule in that respect is—What God has spoken, and what has been accepted by the Church as the word of God, by that, and that only, are we bound in doctrine.[7]

In their encounters with anti-Mormon critics, quite often the Saints seem to feel constrained to defend too much. For example, the fact that Orson Pratt may have said such and such on this or that occasion does not make it a proposition that needs defending. Elder Pratt was very outspoken in his opinions, which sometimes disagreed with the opinions of other General Authorities. He was frequently instructed to make clear to his hearers or readers that his views were his own and not the doctrine of the Church; and on at least one occasion he was instructed by the President of the Church to recant publicly opinions he had represented as doctrine.[8]

Yet time and again the private opinions or even the half-serious speculations of Orson Pratt and others are presented in the literature of the anti-Mormons as mainstream LDS doctrine. The problem is compounded by some enthusiastic Latter-day Saints who themselves will not observe this distinction and insist on teaching the personal opinions and speculations of past leaders as though they were the official doctrines of the Church.

Now, none of this should be taken to mean that in matters of administration within the LDS church the General Authorities are not inspired or that they must submit every policy decision to the members for a sustaining vote. The revelations recorded in the Doctrine and Covenants, *already accepted* as binding by the Church, along with the ordination to their callings give the Brethren the keys and authority to administer the affairs of the Church as the Lord may direct without their needing a sustaining vote for each individual decision.[9] Thus the Church in conference sustains only the individuals who hold the keys, but does not need to sustain separately every detail of their administration. Consequently the policies and procedures of the Church are ''official'' and ''inspired'' whenever those holding the keys of that ministry unitedly declare them to be so. Similarly the revelations already accepted by the Church give to the General Authorities and to many others the right to ''preach, teach, expound, exhort,''—that is, to interpret and apply *existing* doctrines within the context of their individual stewardships. The Brethren need no further license or sustaining vote to interpret, define, and apply the doctrines of the Church, or to administer the affairs of the Church and dictate its policies and procedures, than to be sustained in conference as prophets, seers, and revelators and as duly ordained members of their respective quorums.

Latter-day Saints believe that the General Authorities receive inspiration and revelation from God constantly in the administration of the affairs of the Church. They also believe that individuals within the Church may receive personal revelation, even on doctrinal matters, for their private benefit. When doctrinal revelation is given to such individuals, however, the Lord commands them to keep it to themselves (see Alma 12:9). Such revelation is not for the Church generally, but for that individual alone. No *new* doctrine is binding as the official doctrine of the Church unless it has been received by the President of the Church and until it has been sustained by the Church in general conference.

Finally, from an LDS point of view some things may be correct without being official Church doctrine. For example, it is probably true that the sum of the squares of the sides of a right triangle is equal to the square of its hypotenuse, but the Pythagorean theorem has never been sustained in a general conference of the Church. Similarly the doctrinal opinions of individual

Latter-day Saints could very well turn out to be correct—and some such opinions are believed by many of the Saints —but that does not make them the official doctrine of the Church. This category of things that *may* be true and that are believed by some in the Church is confusing to members and nonmembers alike. Hence the Brethren have insisted again and again that the members avoid such speculative matters and teach only from the standard works, for only they contain the official doctrines of the Church.

For all of these reasons the only valid judgments of whether or not LDS doctrine is Christian must be based on the official doctrines of the Church, interpreted as the Latter-day Saints interpret them.

Anomalies

Yet another way in which anti-Mormon critics often misrepresent LDS doctrine is in the presentation of anomalies as though they were the doctrine of the Church. Anomalies occur in every field of human endeavor, even in science. An anomaly is something unexpected that cannot be explained by the existing laws or theories, but which does not constitute evidence for changing the laws and theories. An anomaly is a glitch.

For example, if a chemist combines two parts hydrogen and one part oxygen a hundred times in a row, and ninety-nine times she gets water but on the hundredth time she gets alcohol, this does not mean that one percent of the time the laws of chemistry are different. It simply means that something was wrong with the hundredth experiment, even though the experimenter may not know what it was. Beakers may have been mislabelled; grad students may have been playing a practical joke; instruments might have given incorrect readings; secretaries might have typed the wrong information. If the anomaly could be reproduced experimentally, then it would be significant and would demand a change in the theories. But if it can't be reproduced, it is simply ignored—as an anomaly. It is assumed that some unknown factor was different in the case of the anomalous results, and the experiment yielding those results is therefore invalid. Moreover, to ignore such anomalies is not considered dishonesty, but represents sound scientific method.

Just as there are anomalies in the world of science, there are anomalies in the realm of history. By historical anomalies in the LDS tradition I do not mean doctrines that are little known or seldom taught. Mormonism has both, but these are not anomalies. By LDS anomalies I mean reported statements of leaders of the Church that cannot be understood *even by the Church*, and that cannot be reconciled to the official doctrines of the Church. These reported statements may disagree with the belief and practice of the Church (then and now), with subsequent scientific findings, with the statements of other prophets, or even with the stated view of the same prophet on other occasions. With anomalies the question is not whether to believe the prophet; the question is, What proposition is being presented here for our belief?

For many Christian churches the text of 1 Corinthians 15:29 presents such an anomaly: "Else what shall they do which are baptized for the dead, if the dead rise not at all? why are they then baptized for the dead?" For most churches it's not a question of whether to believe Paul on the subject of baptism for the dead; it's a question of knowing exactly what Paul meant by this cryptic reference. Since the Bible gives no further information on the subject, many conclude that they just don't know enough about what Paul meant to formulate a doctrine, and so they set the passage aside as an anomaly. "Whatever Paul intended was undoubtedly correct," they say. "We just aren't sure we know what he intended."

The Adam-God Theory

A classic example of an anomaly in the LDS tradition is the so-called "Adam-God theory." During the latter half of the nineteenth century Brigham Young made some remarks about the relationship between Adam and God that the Latter-day Saints have never been able to understand. The reported statements conflict with LDS teachings before and after Brigham Young, as well as with statements of President Young himself during the same period of time. So how do Latter-day Saints deal with the phenomenon? We don't; we simply set it aside. It is an anomaly. On occasion my colleagues and I at Brigham Young University have tried to figure out what Brigham Young might have actually said and what it might have meant, but the attempts have always failed. The reported statements simply do not compute — we cannot make sense out of them. This is not a matter of believing it or disbelieving it; we simply don't know what "it" is. If Brigham

Young were here we could ask him what he actually said and what he meant by it, but he is not here, and even expert students of his thought are left to wonder whether he was misquoted, whether he meant to say one thing and actually said another, whether he was somehow joking with or testing the Saints, or whether some vital element that would make sense out of the reports has been omitted.

For the Latter-day Saints, however, the point is moot, since whatever Brigham Young said, true or false, was never presented to the Church for a sustaining vote. It was not then and is not now a doctrine of the Church, and—like the chemist who can neither explain nor reproduce her results—the Church has merely set the phenomenon aside as an anomaly.

Nevertheless anti-Mormon critics have not only interpreted Brigham Young's remarks; they have also elevated their own interpretation, the "Adam-God theory," to the status of official LDS doctrine. Once again our theology is being dictated to us by our critics. According to them Brigham Young taught that Adam, the husband of Eve and father of Cain, is identical to that Elohim who is God, the Father of spirits and the Father of Jesus Christ. But for Latter-day Saints this interpretation has always been simply impossible. It contradicts the LDS scriptures; it contradicts the teachings of Joseph Smith; it contradicts other statements by Brigham Young made during the same period of time; it contradicts the teachings of all the prophets since Brigham Young; and it contradicts the sacred ordinances of the LDS temples, with which Brigham Young was intimately familiar.

The point is that while anti-Mormons can believe whatever they want, the Latter-day Saints have never believed that Brigham Young taught the "Adam-God theory" as explained in anti-Mormon literature, and that whether Brigham Young believed it or not, the "Adam-God theory" as proposed and interpreted by non-Mormons simply cannot be found in the theology of the Latter-day Saints. I do not believe it; my parents do not believe it; and neither did their parents before them. Yet there are few anti-Mormon publications that do not present this "Adam-God theory," the doctrinal creation of our opponents, as one of the most characteristic doctrines of the Latter-day Saints. This is certainly misrepresentation; I believe it is also dishonest; and when used to justify a charge that Latter-day Saints aren't Christians, it is another example of condemning the Latter-day Saints for things they do not believe or teach.

Summary

In summary, the Latter-day Saints cannot be judged to be non-Christian for things they do *not* believe, whether these things are fabrications, distortions, or anomalies. The doctrine of the Latter-day Saints is clearly defined and readily accessible to all. Doctrines are official if they are found in the standard works of the Church (the Bible, the Book of Mormon, the Doctrine and Covenants, and the Pearl of Great Price) or if they are sustained by the Church in general conference. Policies and procedures are official when those who hold the keys of that ministry and who have been sustained by the Church declare them to be the official policies and procedures of the Church. Other denominations claim the right to define and interpret their own doctrines and policies. Surely the Latter-day Saints must be accorded the same privilege.

3

The Exclusion by Name-Calling

In textbooks dealing with logical thinking the ad hominem fallacy is described as indulging in name-calling rather than actually answering an opponent's arguments. *Ad hominem* is Latin for "against the man," and an ad hominem argument focuses on the emotions and prejudices felt toward a person or group rather than on the logic of their arguments. Ad hominem arguments can be quite effective at winning support for an otherwise weak position by obscuring the real issues involved. Name-calling has often been used in religious controversies. Catholics called Protestants "heretics"; Protestants called Catholics "Papists"; both called Jews "Christ killers"; and all three have been labelled "infidels" by Muslims. But intellectually speaking the ad hominem tactic amounts to nothing more than saying, "Boo for your religion, and hurrah for mine."

The LDS Church as a "Cult"

The nasty name most frequently flung at The Church of Jesus Christ of Latter-day Saints by its detractors is "cult." Undoubtedly the term is meant to call up images of Druids burning captives alive in wicker baskets, of painted priests flinging virgins into volcanoes, or of satanic rituals performed in the dark of the moon. When critics call the LDS church a "cult," the implied

logic seems to be that there are objective criteria for distinguishing "cults" from "religions," and that since Mormonism is a
"cult" and Christianity is a "religion," Mormons can't be Christians. One flaw in this logic is that there are in fact no such objective criteria for distinguishing cults from religions, as a quick look
at *Webster's Third New International Dictionary* will show. There the
pertinent definitions under the entry "cult" are as follows:

> 1: religious practice: worship 2: a system of beliefs and
> ritual connected with the worship of a deity, a spirit, or a
> group of deities or spirits 3a: the rites, ceremonies, and
> practices of a religion: the formal aspect of religious experi-
> ence b *Roman Catholicism:* reverence and ceremonial vener-
> ation paid to God or to the Virgin Mary or to the saints or
> to objects that symbolize or otherwise represent them 4: a
> religion regarded as unorthodox or spurious; *also:* a minor-
> ity religious group holding beliefs regarded as unorthodox
> or spurious: sect.[1]

One can clearly see that in definitions 1, 2, and 3 there is no distinction between a cult and a religion — the terms are in fact quite
synonymous. It is only definition 4 that comes close to the meaning desired by anti-Mormons. Use of the term *cult* in this latter
sense, however, says nothing objective about a religion itself.
Such language merely communicates a speaker's negative evalu-
ation of the religion in question. With its negative connotations
the term *cult* does not describe what a religion *is*, only how it is *regarded*, and simply means "a religion [usually one smaller or
newer than mine] that I don't like." It is a word that communicates information about the speaker rather than about the thing
described. *Cult* is therefore a totally subjective rather than objective term. To both the pagans and the Jews, earliest Christianity
was a "cult," but this says nothing objective about Christianity
except that it was disliked by those who so described it. There is
no objective definition for the word *cult* in standard English that
does what the anti-Mormons want it to do.

Nevertheless there have been many attempts to define *cult* in
an objective way without losing the term's negative connotations. So far all these attempts have failed. Let us take, for example, the last and most ambitious definition proposed by the
late Walter Martin. I single out this one only because, from a
non-Mormon view, Martin is certainly the consensus expert on
this subject, and in his latest and longest definition of *cult* he

renders his most complete explanation of the term. In his proposed objective definition Martin lists ten characteristics common to cults which he believes distinguish them from legitimate religions.[2] At the conclusion of his list the author assures the reader that "we have presented here *all* of the essential marks which distinguish many of the new cults from the rest of society and from the biblical Christian church."[3]

The flaw, however, in the proposed definition — and the Achilles' heel for all such definitions of *cult* — is that any objective definition of *cult* that can be applied to The Church of Jesus Christ of Latter-day Saints can *also* be applied to the Christian church of the New Testament and to most of today's mainline denominations when they were in their infancy. Let's examine Martin's ten points one at a time.

1. "Cults, new as well as old, are usually started by strong and dynamic leaders who are in complete control of their followers."

Certainly Jesus Christ must be reckoned a strong and dynamic leader. Is there any doubt that Jesus was in complete control of his followers, or that the disciples would have done anything for him, including the giving of their lives? Jesus asked his followers to give up everything (see Matthew 19:27–29; 16:24–26), and on occasion refused permission to his disciples even to carry out social obligations to their families (Luke 9:57–62). Was New Testament Christianity a "cult" because Jesus was a strong and dynamic leader in complete control of his followers?

2. "All cults possess some Scripture that is either added to or which replaces the Bible as God's Word."

A major claim of the early Christian church was that the new covenant of the gospel and the New Testament that records it superseded the old covenant of the law of Moses and the Old Testament that records it (Galatians 3:24–29; Hebrews 8:7–13; 10:8–9). To the scriptures accepted during Jesus' lifetime as the word of God the Christians *added* at least four Gospels, a book of Acts, twenty-one Epistles, and an Apocalypse. The Jews were just as incensed at these spurious (from their point of view) additions to God's word in the period of the early Church as anti-Mormon critics are at the Book of Mormon today. Since the early Christians both added books to the previously accepted canon of scripture and insisted that the New Testament fulfilled and superseded the Old, this is another indication, using Walter Martin's definition, that early Christianity was a "cult."

3. "The new cults have rigid standards for membership and accept no members who will not become integrally involved in the group."

According to Jesus, "strait is the gate, and narrow is the way, which leadeth unto life, and few there be that find it" (Matthew 7:14). The Apostle Paul warned the Corinthian Christians that "if any man that is called a brother be a fornicator, or covetous, or an idolater, or a railer, or a drunkard, or an extortioner; with such an one no not to eat. . . . Therefore put away from among yourselves that wicked person." (1 Corinthians 5:11, 13.) Apparently the conditions for fellowship at Corinth were fairly strict. Paul went on to tell the Corinthians that "neither fornicators, nor idolaters, nor adulterers, nor effeminate, nor abusers of themselves with mankind, nor thieves, nor covetous, nor drunkards, nor revilers, nor extortioners, shall inherit the kingdom of God" (1 Corinthains 6:9–10). Surely if insistence upon high standards makes a religious movement a "cult," then early Christianity qualifies.

Furthermore, if insisting that members become integrally involved in the group is characteristic of "cults," what shall we do with Paul's demand in 2 Corinthians 6:14, 15, and 17? "Be ye not unequally yoked together with unbelievers: for what fellowship hath righteousness with unrighteousness? and what communion hath light with darkness? And what concord hath Christ with Belial? or what part hath he that believeth with an infidel? . . . Wherefore come out from among them, and be ye separate, saith the Lord, and touch not the unclean thing; and I will receive you."

It is hard for me to understand how anyone versed in the New Testament could believe that Jesus did not require a high standard of righteousness of his followers, or that he found a partial commitment to his gospel as acceptable as a total commitment. The evidence to the contrary is overwhelming. But because early Christianity demanded high standards and a total commitment, was it therefore a "cult"?

4. "Cultists often become members of one cult after membership in one or more other cults."

This part of the definition is circular, since you already have to know what a cult is before you can use the term. Even so, let us consider it briefly in an ancient context. From the viewpoint of the Jews and Romans both the movement of John the Baptist and that of Jesus were "cults." John 1:35–37 tells us that two of the disciples of John the Baptist later became disciples of Jesus, and it is likely that many others did as well. According to Martin's reasoning, this change of affiliation could indicate they were cultists.

5. "The new cults are actively evangelistic and spend much of their time in proselytizing new converts."

According to Matthew 28:19–20, after his resurrection Jesus told his disciples: "Go ye therefore, and teach all nations, baptizing them in the name of the Father, and of the Son, and of the Holy Ghost: teaching them to observe all things whatsoever I have commanded you." The Apostle Paul certainly spent "much of [his] time in proselytizing new converts." Again the New Testament Church qualifies as a cult under this definition.

6. "Often we find that the leaders or officials of the new cults are not professional clergymen."

The Jewish high priests noticed this very thing about Peter and John, "that they were unlearned and ignorant men" (Acts 4:13). Jesus was a carpenter by trade; and Peter, James, and John were fishermen.

7. "All the new cults have a system of doctrine and practice which is in some state of flux."

Flux is a relative term. During the forty-day period following the resurrection of Jesus, the Apostles certainly learned a lot of new things that they hadn't known from the beginnings in Galilee (Acts 1:3). Some years after the resurrection of Jesus, Peter received a vision changing the Christian attitude toward Gentiles and the role of the law of Moses (Acts 10). Paul's private opinions about remarriage became Christian doctrine and biblical teaching in 1 Corinthians 7:6–9, 12, 25, 40. In New Testament times the Church held a council to decide whether Gentiles needed to be circumcised (Acts 15); and beyond the New Testament period "orthodox" Christianity held many councils to determine or to clarify its doctrines and policies, from the Council of Nicaea to the Second Vatican Council in our own century. All of these councils settled questions neither asked nor answered in the Bible. Was Christianity "in flux" and a "cult" because its earliest leaders continued to receive revelations even after the ascension of Christ, or because the later church was still working out its view of the relationship between the Father, Son, and Holy Ghost centuries after the death of Jesus?

8. "In harmony with Christian theology, the new cults all believe that there is continual, ongoing communication from

God. However, the cults differ from the biblical Christian church in believing that their new 'revelations' can contradict and even at times supersede God's first revelation, the Bible.''

According to Walter Martin the contradiction of previous revelation by new revelation is a sure sign of a cult. Yet God has often given one commandment to his children at one time and then later replaced it with another. He did this to Abraham merely to test him (Genesis 22:2, 12). But the best example of God exercising his prerogative to command and then revoke comes in the case of the law of Moses, given to Israel by God and recorded in the Bible. This law was both contradicted (compare Genesis 17:7, 14 with Galatians 5:1–4) and superseded (Galatians 3:24–29; Hebrews 8:7–13; 10:8–9) by later revelation. The early Christians simply believed that although God had spoken once upon Sinai and had given them scriptures, he now spoke to them again and had given new revelations that superseded the old ones. Many Jews continue to be scandalized that Christians, who worship the God of Israel, could ignore the law given to Israel on Sinai.

9. ''The new cults claim to have truth not available to any other groups or individuals.''

On one occasion, when many were offended at Jesus and were leaving him, the Savior turned to the Twelve and asked if they would also go away. Peter responded, ''Lord, to whom shall we go? thou hast the words of eternal life.'' (John 6:66–68.) The early Christians knew that there wasn't any other source for divine truth but Jesus. Jesus himself said, ''I am the way, the truth, and the life: no man cometh unto the Father, but by me'' (John 14:6). In other words, Jesus offered to the early Christian church ''truth not available to any other groups or individuals'' from any other source. Again early Christianity qualifies as a cult under the proposed definition.

10. ''The last major characteristic of the new cults concerns cultic vocabulary. Each cult has an initiate vocabulary by which it describes the truths of its revelation. Sometimes the 'in words' of a particular cult are the words of orthodox Christianity, but invested with new meanings. . . . At other times the cult may coin new words or phrases.''

Much of the vocabulary of the New Testament Church came from Judaism. Some of the vocabulary retained its Jewish meaning (for example, *Messiah* and *resurrection*), but many of the old words (such as *Israel, covenant,* and *grace*) were defined and used in new ways. Older Jewish practices were given new meanings: the

Sabbath meal became the Lord's Supper; the Jewish purification rite became Christian baptism; the Sabbath became the Lord's Day. Eventually new terms were coined, such as *Millennium, Advent, Second Coming,* or *Trinity.*

Thus we see that out of the ten characteristics proposed as objective criteria for identifying "cults," the early Christian Church manifests all ten—a perfect score. What does this tell us? Only that as an objective means of distinguishing false "cults" from legitimate "religions" the proposed definition fails, not because it's badly done but because what it attempts to do cannot be done. The word *cult,* used with negative connotations, is simply not an objective term, and attempts to make it such lead to absurd conclusions: by the ten-point definition proposed above, early Christianity was a "cult."

Now, certainly there are religions that many outsiders dislike, and we might all agree to call these religions "cults," but the label still describes only our common opinion of that religion and not the religion itself. There are simply no objective criteria for distinguishing religions from "cults."

Summary

To summarize, *cult* is a subjective word meaning, to the particular person using it, "a religion I don't like." When someone refers to The Church of Jesus Christ of Latter-day Saints as a "cult," that simply tells us that the speaker doesn't like the Church. Christianity itself was once a new religion with dynamic leadership, strong in-group bonding, high moral expectations, and additional scriptures, all of which greatly offended the mainline religions of its day. Its leaders were not professionally trained clergy, but they did attempt to convert the world to a truth no one else had. By most of the objective definitions that have been proposed for the term *cult,* early Christianity was one. And so far any general definition of a cult that would fit the Latter-day Saints will also fit New Testament Christianity. But that's not bad company to be in.

4

The Historical or Traditional Exclusion

Modern Christian orthodoxy often sees itself as properly consisting of not only the events and doctrines revealed in the New Testament but also the historical, theological, and traditional developments of later centuries. It is sometimes argued that in order to be truly Christian modern churches must accept both biblical Christianity *and* the traditional Christianity that grew out of it. This, in a nutshell, is the historical exclusion. If one does not accept the centuries of historical development and elaboration—the councils, creeds, and customs, the theologians and the philosophers—in addition to the biblical doctrines, then one is not a true Christian. According to this view the biblical revelation taken alone is inadequate for true Christianity.

This type of exclusionary thinking is illustrated by an incident that occurred to me while I was in graduate school. I had been invited by one of the large Protestant churches in town to teach a lesson on the beliefs and practices of the Latter-day Saints. Some of my professors were members of that church, and I was very pleased when they attended my lecture. At the end of the lesson I bore testimony to the restored gospel, to the divine call of the Prophet Joseph Smith, and most of all to the saving work of Jesus Christ.

When I was done one of my professors raised his hand and said, "Well, Steve, that was wonderful and informative, but I think you have left us with the incorrect impression that you Mormons are a Christian denomination, when, of course, you are not." Now, I knew this man fairly well, and consequently I knew what he meant by this statement. It was not a malicious pronouncement, but it had absolutely nothing to do with what Latter-day Saints believed or didn't believe about Jesus Christ. The man was a liberal Protestant historian, and his definition of the term *Christian* was a *historical* definition; it had nothing to do with personal belief. To him a Christian was someone whose theological family tree could be traced back through the Protestant Reformation, through the Roman Catholic church, and through the ecumenical councils to the first council of bishops at Nicaea in A.D. 325. His definition had very little to do with *what* one believed; it was more concerned with *how* one came by that belief. In his view, if your theology had the right pedigree you were a Christian; if not, though you might believe every word of the New Testament, you were still not a true Christian, because your intellectual and theological genealogy were all wrong.

As a liberal Protestant historian this professor had additional incentives for defining *Christian* in terms of heritage rather than belief, for, as I knew from private conversations with him, he did not personally believe most of the supernatural claims of the primitive Christian church. If "being Christian" was a matter of heritage rather than of personal belief, he could still claim the title "Christian" as his own, even though he did not believe the historical claims of the New Testament.

Thus, being aware of the background of this professor and his views, I understood what he meant when he said, "Mormons aren't Christians," but I also was aware that the congregation did *not* understand his meaning correctly. To them it sounded as if he were denying that the Latter-day Saints believed in Jesus Christ. And so for their benefit I initiated the following exchange:

"Do you personally believe that Jesus Christ was the literal Son of God, that he had no mortal father?" I asked.

"No," he replied, "not literally."

"Do you believe in the divinity of the historical Jesus?"

"No."

"Do you believe that Jesus had the power to perform miracles?"

"No."

"Do you believe that he took upon him the sins of the world in some literal way, as a real transfer of real guilt?"

"No."

"Do you believe that in some literal way Jesus died for us?"

"No."

"Do you believe in the literal, bodily resurrection of Jesus?"

"No."

"Do you believe in a final judgment?"

"No."

"Do you believe in an afterlife at all?"

"I think so."

"And are you a Christian?"

"Of course I am."

"How can you say that?"

"Because I accept the New Testament as containing God's word, even though I do not interpret it literally, and because I am an ordained minister in a denomination that traces its Christian heritage back to the New Testament period without a historical break."

"All right, now, as a Latter-day Saint I believe that Jesus Christ is the literal Son of God; that he was and is divine; that he had the power to work miracles; that he took the sins of the world upon him in Gethsemane and on Calvary; that he died for us; that he was literally, bodily raised up on the third day; and that he will raise us up to judgment and a glorious afterlife. Now, am I a Christian?"

"Absolutely not."

"Why not?"

"Because you are a member of a church that is not theologically derived from and dependent upon the councils and creeds of the historical church, and because you reject traditional Christianity and its theology after the second century."

"Does your definition of 'being Christian' have anything to do with my personal belief in Jesus Christ?"

"No."

Now, when it was laid out like this, the congregation could see that the man was using a specialized definition of the term *Christian*, and consequently that he was not really saying what they had at first thought. After the lecture several people approached me to say that according to how they defined "being a Christian," the Latter-day Saints certainly qualified, but that they weren't so sure anymore about the professor.

To the extent that the historical exclusion offers a specialized or nonstandard definition of *Christian*, it is merely another form of the exclusion by definition and suffers from the same fallacy (see chapter 1 herein). The historical exclusion, however, involves additional considerations that ought to be examined here.

The Great Apostasy

First of all, it should be noted that the Latter-day Saints do reject the authority of traditional Christianity after the death of the New Testament Apostles. In the LDS view the keys and authority promised to Peter in Matthew 16:16 were *apostolic* in nature, and therefore when the Apostles were gone, so were their keys and authority. Thereafter, people could still be "Christian" in the generic sense, and are not, in the LDS view, automatically excluded from salvation (there will be opportunities to accept the gospel in the postmortal life); but the historical church no longer possessed the fulness of the gospel. This is the LDS doctrine of the Great Apostasy, a doctrine which is also taught in the New Testament. Following are two examples from the teachings of Paul:

> Now we beseech you, brethren, by the coming of our Lord Jesus Christ, and by our gathering together unto him,
>
> That ye be not soon shaken in mind, or be troubled, neither by spirit, nor by word, nor by letter as from us, as that the day of Christ is at hand.
>
> Let no man deceive you by any means: for that day shall not come, except there come a falling away [Greek *apostasia*] first, and that man of sin be revealed, the son of perdition;
>
> Who opposeth and exalteth himself above all that is called God, or that is worshipped; so that he as God sitteth in the temple of God, shewing himself that he is God.
>
> Remember ye not, that, when I was yet with you, I told you these things? (2 Thessalonians 2:1–5.)

> For I know this, that after my departing shall grievous wolves enter in among you, not sparing the flock.
>
> Also of your own selves shall men arise, speaking perverse things, to draw away disciples after them.
>
> Therefore watch, and remember, that by the space of three years I ceased not to warn every one night and day with tears. (Acts 20:29–31.)

These passages, and others that might be cited,[1] tell us not only that Paul was concerned about an inevitable coming apostasy, but also that he spent a great deal of energy warning the Church about it. It is the LDS belief that such an apostasy actually took place and that the keys and authority of the Apostles were lost.

For this reason Latter-day Saints reject the binding authority of subsequent developments in historical Christianity.

Christians with Similar Views

It is surprising that Protestants would criticize the Latter-day Saints for believing in an apostasy and rejecting subsequent developments, since Protestants have essentially done the same thing—only instead of rejecting the authority of the traditional church after the first century, they reject it after the fifteenth. Protestant Reformers used many of the same Bible passages cited above to prove that the Roman church was corrupt and to justify their own attempts at reform. Martin Luther and others went so far as to identify the pope as the Antichrist.[2] If some Protestants argue that Mormons aren't Christians because they reject the Council of Nicaea (A.D. 325), couldn't Catholics argue that Protestants aren't Christians because they reject the Council of Trent (A.D. 1545–47)? The issue here does not involve a difference in kind but only of degree or of timing. Thus, in terms of the doctrine of an apostasy—that is, that at some point in time the historical church was no longer the true Church—most Protestants agree with the Latter-day Saints in principle; they just differ on the dates.

Most Protestants accept as doctrinally valid and binding only the first seven of the great ecumenical councils, the last of which, the Second Council of Nicaea, was held in A.D. 787.[3] Greek Orthodoxy formally rejected the authority of the Western church in A.D. 1054, although their differences began long before this date. Six centuries earlier Armenian, Syrian, Coptic, and Abyssinian Christianity all rejected the "great church" at the Council of Chalcedon (A.D. 451), and have been separate churches ever since; hence we might ask, If the historical exclusion is applied to these "orthodox" churches—which accept only three of the twenty-one ecumenical councils—can they still be considered Christians? And if the Armenians, Syrians, Abyssinians, and Copts can reject everything in traditional Christianity from the fifty century on and still be Christians, then where is the cutoff that marks how much can be rejected? If it can be as early as the fifth century, then why not as early as the second?

Thus some denominations place their break with the traditional church[4] at A.D. 451, while others might put it at 787, 1054, or 1517. Regardless of who was right and who was wrong in any of the schisms, in each case *somebody* was rejecting the authority of a mother church and refusing to be bound by its traditions and doctrines. Yet no one seriously accuses the Armenians, Copts, Syrians, Greek Orthodox, or Protestants of being non-Christian for having done this.

Catholics often think of Protestants as having rejected true Christianity, while Protestants think of themselves as having recovered the true Christianity from which the Roman church had wandered. For the purposes of my argument it doesn't matter who is right; what matters is that while rejecting each other's traditions and doctrines, Protestants and Catholics still call each other Christians in the generic sense. Why, then, cannot the Latter-day Saints, who believe in Jesus Christ and who accept the New Testament witness, also reject later traditions and doctrines without being labelled non-Christian?

A Single Christian Tradition?

Moreover, Protestants differ among themselves in the amount of the accumulated Christian heritage they accept. Many Protestants don't venerate the saints, or observe Lent, or know that Saint Swithin's Day is July 15. Is there some critical percentage of the nonbiblical traditions that must be believed, some specific amount of the accumulated customs that one must accept in order to be a true Christian, so that by accepting 50 percent, say, of the postbiblical material one is a Christian, but not with 49 percent? Or are there certain key nonbiblical traditions that must be accepted, such as observing Easter on the right day, while other trivial traditions may be safely ignored, such as eating fish on Friday? And exactly who decides which customs are dispensable and which ones are not, and by what authority do they do so, if the traditions are admittedly nonbiblical to begin with? Who preserves the *real* postbiblical "Christian tradition," the Greek Orthodox monks at the Mar Saba monastery or the faith-healing, TV evangelist from Texas?

What exactly is *the* Christian tradition, and how can Mormons be expected to accept it, when mainline Christians disagree among themselves on virtually every aspect of it? In the words of David Steinmetz, Kearns Professor of the History of Christianity at Duke University: "Christians have argued, often passionately, over every conceivable point of Christian doctrine from the filioque[5] to the immaculate conception. There is scarcely an issue of worship, theology, ethics, and politics over which some Christians have not disagreed among themselves."[6]

Like the modern Latter-day Saints, the Puritans rejected any practice or custom from the Christian tradition that could not be found in the New Testament. And according to Kenneth Scott Latourette, the Seekers, among them Roger Williams and George Fox,[7] "held that Antichrist had ruled so long that no true churches or valid office-holders existed and could not until God sent apostles to establish and ordain new ones."[8] Now, this is very similar to the Latter-day Saint view. Does this make these venerable Protestants non-Christians? Remember, the question here isn't whether their belief was correct; rather, the question is, If the Puritans, Separatists (among them our own Pilgrim Fathers), and Seekers can utterly reject the historical Christian tradition beyond the warrant of the New Testament and still be Christians, why can't the Latter-day Saints?

A Pure Christian Tradition?

Another problem with insisting that one must accept the historical Christian heritage in order to be a Christian is that many of the present traditions and customs in that heritage were originally pagan practices that have been "Christianized."[9] The Puritans in colonial America opposed the celebration of Christmas because they could find no biblical warrant for the practice, and attributed it to paganism and "popery."[10] Most of the customary symbols of Christmas — such as the Christmas tree, candles, holly, mistletoe, yule log, and so on — were adopted from the pagan religions of northern Europe, and the traditional date for celebrating Christmas was originally that of the pagan Roman festival of *Natalis Solis Invicti* (the Birthday of the Invincible Sun-god).[11]

In addition, much pagan influence came into the Christian church in connection with the veneration of the saints. For example, did Saint George *really* slay a dragon? Most scholars identify his legend with the Baltic and Slavic gods Kalvis and Kresnik, and with the Greek myth of Perseus and Andromeda.[12] In many places local Christian festivals, especially those occurring on the solstices and equinoxes, are merely continuations of pre-Christian celebrations now dressed up in Christian trappings; and many a local pagan deity has continued to be worshipped in the guise of a Christian saint, and so has become part of the Christian heritage. Must one, in order to be a true Christian, accept those parts of the Christian heritage that originated in paganism in postbiblical times?

The Doctrinal Tradition

Now, one might respond that it is not the *customs* and *traditions* of the historical church that must be accepted after all, but only the *doctrines* of the historical councils and creeds. But if the councils and creeds teach doctrines not found in the New Testament, on what authority must they be accepted? And if the councils and creeds merely repeat or summarize the doctrines of the New Testament without adding to them, then why is it necessary to accept them *in addition* to the New Testament itself? Only by making the councils the primary sources of Christian doctrine and the New Testament scriptures secondary can the historical exclusion work, even theoretically. And if other churches argue that it is necessary for Latter-day Saints to accept the councils in order to be Christian, then we might well ask, *Which* councils must be accepted? How can these other churches themselves accept only three, or four, or seven, and not all twenty-one? In actuality many denominations reject *some* of the councils for the same reasons that the Latter-day Saints reject them *all*—because they add to and conflict with the New Testament gospel as the Holy Spirit leads us to understand it.

The Latter-day Saints believe, and modern scholarship agrees, that the theology of the councils and creeds represents a radical change from the theology of the New Testament Church.[13] The Latter-day Saints see this change between the first and fourth centuries as part of a great apostasy; scholars refer to it as the Hellenization of Christianity, meaning the modification of the Christian message into forms that would be acceptable in the gentile Greek cultural world. But in that process of modification and adaptation, Christian teaching became Greek teaching, and Christian theology became Greek philosophy. In the LDS view the admixture of Greek elements with the original message of the gospel did not improve it but diluted it. The resulting historical church was still generically Christian, but was no longer the pure, true Church of the New Testament period.

To a large extent the councils were an attempt to reconcile the simple statements of the scriptures with the philosophical requirements of Greek thinking, and to this extent they represent the conversion of Christianity to Hellenism. According to Maurice Wiles, "all Christian thinking, and especially all Christian thinking about the being and nature of God, was influenced, often unconsciously, by philosophical ideas current in the Hellenistic world."[14]

Concerning this Hellenization of Christianity, the great Anglican scholar Edwin Hatch noted as early as 1888, in a work that is still a classic, that "a large part of what are sometimes called Christian doctrines, and many usages which have prevailed and continue to prevail in the Christian Church, are in reality Greek theories and Greek usages changed in form and colour by the influence of primitive Christianity, but in their essence Greek still."[15]

At a later time this adopted Greek element in the Christian tradition would lead to the condemnation of Galileo by the religious authority of the church—not because his theories conflicted with the Bible, but because they conflicted with Aristotle, and no distinction was then being made between Greek philosophy and biblical Christianity. Now, in modern times, though the traditional church has been forced by science to give up its Greek cosmology, it still clings tenaciously to its Greek theology. Hatch insightfully observed:

> The habit of defining and of making inferences from definitions, grew the more as the philosophers passed over into the Christian lines, and logicians and metaphysicians presided over Christian churches. The speculations which were then agreed upon became stamped as a body of truth, and with the still deeper speculations of the Councils of Constantinople and Chalcedon, the resolutions of the Nicene Fathers have come to be looked upon as almost a new revelation, and the rejection of them as a greater bar to Christian fellowship than the rejection of the New Testament itself.[16]

This is exactly what has happened to the Latter-day Saints. When the historical exclusion is used against them, their acceptance of the New Testament is outweighed by their rejection of the Greek philosophical theology. While rejection of the literal truth of the New Testament witness is seen as a trivial thing or at least as a negotiable issue in many modern Christian denominations, rejection of the philosophical tradition created by the Hellenized church is another matter—*that*, for the excluders, puts the Latter-day Saints outside the Christian pale. Thus, under the historical exclusion the Latter-day Saints are accused of being "non-Christian" not because they reject the biblical Christ and his church, but because they commit the more serious "sin" of rejecting the philosophers. In much of modern Christianity the message of Christ and the message of Plato have become practically indistinguishable.

One of my revered non-LDS teachers in graduate school, W. D. Davies, once described Mormonism as an attempt to return to Christianity as it was before its Hellenization.[17] While many Protestants attempt to *reform* Christianity by giving up the papacy and returning to the church of the conciliar period (A.D. 325–787), the Latter-day Saints seek to *restore* primitive Christianity by giving up Hellenism and returning to the Church of the New Testament period.

In the Roman Catholic Tradition

It is also surprising to me that some Roman Catholic critics have used the historical exclusion against the Latter-day Saints, even though they no longer use it against Protestants, for in some ways Latter-day Saints are closer to the Catholic tradition than most Protestants are. For example, the Latter-day Saints, like Roman Catholics but unlike many Protestant denominations, accept the necessity of all seven traditional sacraments of the Christian church.[18] Martin Luther accepted only the Lord's Supper and baptism as Christian sacraments and rejected the sacramental character of the other five.

Moreover, Mormons accept the doctrine of apostolic succession, which is rejected by a majority of Protestants today. This doctrine states that the authority given by Christ to Peter in Matthew 16:19 is necessary to the "true" Christian church and must be handed down in a human chain of persons who hold the keys and preside over the Church. In Catholic terms this person is the Pope; in LDS terms he is the President and prophet of the Church. Catholics trace the authority of the pope through what they consider to be an unbroken line of authority that passes through Peter back to Christ himself. The Latter-day Saints trace the authority of their prophet through what they consider to be an unbroken line that passes through Peter back to Christ himself. Peter is a key figure, the "rock," in both traditions.[19] In both traditions Peter is the link between the present Church and the authority of Christ. Whether Mormons are correct in believing that Peter personally bestowed the keys of apostleship upon Joseph Smith and Oliver Cowdery (D&C 27:12) is not the issue. The point is that the *theory* upon which the LDS claim is based is equivalent to the Roman Catholic view: the keys of apostolic authority must be transmitted to the true Church through Peter by the laying on of hands. The authority to act as God's agent—that is, the priesthood—can only be received from someone who already has that authority. Latter-day Saints accept the doctrine of apostolic succession, though our chain has fewer links in it than that claimed by the Roman church. On the other hand, most Protestant denominations deny the need of an apostolic succession at all, and have gone to great lengths to reject the whole concept of divine authority being conferred by ordination.[20]

Most Protestants believe that the scriptures lead to conversion and that at conversion the Holy Ghost automatically confers all necessary priesthood on the believer. This is the doctrine of the "priesthood of all believers," which looks to the Bible rather than to the church or to the priesthood as the ultimate source of Christian authority, and which denies the historical transmission of priesthood through the Roman church. This is why Protestants are satisfied with a *Reformation* of the Roman church along scriptural lines; they see authority as an automatic by-product of right belief.

On the other hand, for those who, like the Latter-day Saints and the Catholics, believe in apostolic succession, any break in the chain would require not merely a *Reformation*, but a *Restoration* of apostolic authority. Though Catholics do not believe such a break has occurred and Latter-day Saints do, both share a common view of the necessity of apostolic succession and hold similar concepts of priesthood and ordination. Since Protestants have cut themselves off from the apostolic succession of the Roman church and claim no subsequent restoration of authority, they are forced to claim authority on other grounds—hence the doctrine of the "priesthood of all believers." As Catholics have known for centuries, the biblical concepts of apostolic keys, priesthood, ordination, and sacraments constitute the Achilles' heel of Protestant theology.

Thus, in the areas of priesthood, ordination, and apostolic succession, the Latter-day Saints are actually more "orthodox" than Protestants, sharing the older, more traditonal view with Roman Catholics. Of course, Catholics reject the validity of LDS claims to apostolic succession, just as Latter-day Saints reject the validity of the Catholic succession. But that, in itself, should not cause either to label the other non-Christian, for surely this disagreement is no more serious than the same dispute between Catholics and Protestants generally—and the latter two parties are still willing to refer to each other as Christians. For example, in 1896 Pope Leo XIII declared in a papal bull, *Apostolicae Curae*, that ordination in the Church of England was invalid, a charge which is extremely irritating to Anglicans.[21] Yet Catholics still think of Anglicans as Christians in the generic sense, even though they are, in the Catholic view, outside the apostolic succession. The point is this: If Catholics can still think of Anglicans as generically Christian, even though the pope has declared them to be outside the chain of apostolic authority; or, indeed, if Catholics can think of as Christians those Protestants who reject the idea of succession altogether; then Catholics cannot consistently exclude the Latter-day Saints from Christendom for merely being outside the apostolic succession claimed by the Roman church.

Were the Twelve Apostles Christians?

Finally, by far the most serious objection to the use of the historical exclusion is that it excludes not only the Latter-day Saints but also the New Testament Saints, including Jesus and his Apostles. If it is argued that one must accept the whole package of traditional Christianity in order to be a Christian—if one cannot merely accept the biblical teachings but must also accept the councils, creeds, and theologians of later centuries—then it is chronologically impossible for Jesus and his church to qualify. Since the New Testament itself, however, refers to the first-century Saints as Christians, by this alone we may know that the historical exclusion is invalid (Acts 11:26; 26:28; 1 Peter 4:16).

In the book of Galatians, Paul argues that the law of Moses cannot be necessary to Christianity, since Abraham was justified by his faith in Christ four hundred years before the law was even given. Paul further argues that if Abraham could be justified by faith without the law, so could those Gentiles who followed Abraham's example. (Galatians 3:6–18.) This is precisely my argument here. Accepting the councils, creeds, and other traditional elaborations of the New Testament religion cannot be a necessary condition to being a Christian, for the New Testament Christians lived four hundred years before the formulation of the

Nicene Creed at the Council of Chalcedon.[22] And if the New Testament Saints could be Christians without the postbiblical traditions, then so can the Latter-day Saints.

One may wish to argue that the Latter-day Saints really don't believe what the New Testament Saints believed, but in that event the objection has shifted ground from a historical exclusion to a doctrinal one, which will be dealt with in a subsequent chapter. There is simply no purely *historical* or *traditional* exclusion that will eliminate the Latter-day Saints from the family of Christian churches that does not also eliminate the Saints of the New Testament.

Summary

In summary, the historical exclusion is invalid because it proposes a nonstandard definition for Christian, a definition that is based not on one's belief in Christ, but on one's cultural and theological pedigree. Also, it is invalid because it is used selectively against the Latter-day Saints, but not against others who have also rejected the traditional church. Many denominations have rejected all or part of an earlier orthodoxy but are still considered to be Christian. Furthermore, the historical exclusion is invalid because it makes the New Testament inadequate for communicating Christian faith unless it is supplemented by later nonbiblical traditions. But most of all, the historical exclusion is invalid because it proposes a test for being Christian (namely, acceptance of the later historical church with its councils, creeds, and customs) that the New Testament Saints themselves could not have passed, having lived centuries before these things came to be.

5

The Canonical or Biblical Exclusion

The Greek word *kanon* means, first of all, a "ruler" or a "straightedge" and, secondarily, a "standard" or "norm." From this second meaning comes the English word *canon*, which means, when referring to the scriptures, "the list of books recognized as authoritative." The canon of scripture, then, is the standard collection of texts accepted by Christians as the word of God, or as authoritative. If a book is said to be canonical or one of the "standard works" (the LDS equivalent of "canonical"), that means it is on the list of approved and accepted scriptural books. For non-Mormons the canon is the list of books that make up the Bible.

It is well known that Latter-day Saints have an expanded canon of scripture compared to the rest of the Christian world. In addition to the Bible, they recognize the Book of Mormon, the Doctrine and Covenants, and the Pearl of Great Price as the word of God. These four collections of inspired writings constitute the standard works, or canon of scripture, of the LDS church. In its simplest form the canonical exclusion, as applied to the Latter-day Saints, maintains that since Mormons have a different canon than the Christian canon, since they add books of scripture to the Christian Bible, Mormons cannot be Christians.

Adding to the Scriptures

One of the arguments that have been offered in support of this exclusion is that the Bible itself forbids any departure from the Christian canon either by addition or subtraction. The passage usually cited in support of this position is Revelation 22:18–19: ''For I testify unto every man that heareth the words of the prophecy of this book, If any man shall add unto these things, God shall add unto him the plagues that are written in this book: and if any man shall take away from the words of the book of this prophecy, God shall take away his part out of the book of life, and out of the holy city, and from the things which are written in this book.''

Since the above passage comes at the end of the last chapter of the last book of the Bible, the naive reader might naturally assume that the phrase ''the book of this prophecy'' refers to the entire Bible, and thus that the scriptures themselves declare the canon closed. This, however, is not the case. First of all, there is no way to know whether Revelation was the last book of the New Testament to be written. Most scholars date its composition at around A.D. 94–95, but most scholars would also date James, 1 and 2 Peter, Jude, the three Epistles of John, and the Gospel of John at about the same time, or even later.[1] If Revelation was not the last book of the New Testament to be written, then obviously Revelation 22:18–19 cannot be understood as a decree closing the canon of scripture.

But it doesn't really matter whether Revelation was written last or not, for the ''book'' that John was writing when he issued his warning was certainly not the whole Bible, but just the book of Revelation. When John wrote Revelation, the Bible as we know it—a standard collection of inspired texts bound all together in one volume—simply did not yet exist. For centuries after John produced his writings, the individual books of the Bible were in circulation singly or in combination with several others, but *never* as a complete Bible. Of the 362 biblical manuscripts known to have been produced before the tenth century A.D., only one has a complete New Testament, and *none* contains the whole Bible.[2] Of the entire corpus of 5,366 known Greek biblical manuscripts, only thirty-four contain the whole Bible, and all thirty-four were written after A.D. 1000.[3] The Bible, as we know and use it in the Christian world today, is one of the blessings of the age of printing; complete Bibles were virtually unknown before Gutenberg. Thus, when John wrote about ''the prophecy of this book," he was not referring to the collection of books bound together in one volume and known as the Bible, but to the book he was then writing, the book of Revelation. Since the Latter-day Saints neither add to nor take away from the text of the book of Revelation, the passage at 22:18–19 does not apply to their acceptance of extrabiblical scriptures.

This, by the way, is the same reason why Christians and Jews need not worry, in a canonical sense, about the commandment found in Deuteronomy 4:1–2: "Now therefore hearken, O Israel, unto the statutes and unto the judgments, which I teach you, for to do them, that ye may live, and go in and possess the land which the Lord God of your fathers giveth you. *Ye shall not add unto the word which I command you, neither shall ye diminish ought from it*, that ye may keep the commandments of the Lord your God which I command you." (Emphasis added.) If Moses' words were understood to have universal application, then Jews, who accept the later prophets and writings, and Christians, who add the New Testament to the Sinai revelation, would be in clear violation of the commandment of God. But obviously Moses was referring here to the specific revelation then being recorded, and did not intend his warning to close the canon of scripture for all time. Like John, Moses applied a local restriction against tampering with what he had just written, not a universal restriction against ever receiving further scripture from God.

Prophets Always Add to the Scriptures

In fact every one of the Old Testament prophets "added" to the words of his predecessors and to the word of God. Any student of the Bible knows that the author of 1 and 2 Chronicles rewrote material already contained in the books of Kings and Samuel, often quoting them verbatim, and that in his revised account he both added to and subtracted from those earlier books.

New Testament Christians, as we have already pointed out, "added" to the scriptures accepted by Jews. Even within the New Testament itself it appears that Matthew and Luke both "added to" and "took away from" the words written by Mark, for according to current biblical scholarship both Matthew and Luke were written after Mark and used Mark as a base text from which to write their own Gospels (that is, it is believed that they added their own material to Mark's and subtracted from his what they didn't want to use).[4] For example, to what was written in Mark's Gospel, Matthew added the story of the Wise Men, the flight to Egypt, and the Sermon on the Mount; he deleted, among other things, the healing of the Capernaum demoniac in Mark 1:23–28. Among the material Luke added to Mark are the birth of John the Baptist and the parables of the good Samaritan and the prodigal son; Luke, the Gentile, usually deleted passages that might offend Gentiles, such as Mark 7:26–27 (compare Matthew 15:22–26), and passages that showed Christians in conflict with civil authorities (this may be why Luke omits the trouble with King Herod at the birth of Jesus).

Yet even if the view of biblical scholars is wrong and Mark did not write first, the fact that the three synoptic Gospels are different but literarily interdependent makes it certain that at least two of the three writers were adding to and/or deleting from the story as told by one of the others — in whatever order they may have written.

If Matthew, Luke, and John can add to the Jewish scriptures with their own books and, in the process, add to the story contained in the Christian Gospel of Mark, and can still be Christians, then, at least in theory, so can Joseph Smith. For the issue in this case is clearly not whether one adds to the canon of scripture — *all* the biblical Apostles and prophets did that — but whether the one who does so has been authorized and commanded by God. It is not necessary to prove here that the scriptures received by Joseph Smith are genuine. To invalidate the canonical exclusion it is only necessary to show that in other circumstances other Apostles and prophets have added to the canon of scripture without ceasing to be Christians. Since there is no biblical statement closing the canon or prohibiting additional revelation, and since Apostles and prophets have in the past added to the canon — even to the Christian canon — without offending God, the canonical exclusion must be invalid. The logic can be expressed like this:

1. No one who adds to the canon of Christian scripture is a Christian.
2. Joseph Smith adds to the canon of Christian scripture.
3. Therefore Joseph Smith is not a Christian.

But, on the other hand,

4. Matthew, Mark, Luke, John, Peter, and Paul also added to the canon of Christian scripture.

5. Yet we *know* that Matthew, Mark, Luke, John, Peter, and Paul are Christians.
6. Therefore premise number 1 (the canonical exclusion) is false.

The question is not whether Joseph Smith, like the New Testament authors, added to the Christian canon, but whether Joseph Smith, like the New Testament authors, had apostolic authority. If he did, then what he added to the biblical scriptures is Christian. Now, one could object that Joseph Smith was *not* a prophet and did not hold apostolic authority, but that is still abandoning the canonical exclusion and retreating to a different argument.

One hidden motivation behind the canonical exclusion is the firm conviction among most non-Mormons that there will *never* be any more Apostles and prophets. If that conviction were true, then it would follow that there could be no additional scriptures, for no one would have the apostolic authority to write them. Latter-day Saints simply deny that the conviction is true, for no biblical warrant can be found for it.

Mormons and Biblical Inerrancy

Another motivation behind the canonical exclusion is the conviction of the excluders that the Bible alone is enough, that the present canon is so perfect, so complete, that it cannot possibly be improved upon. This is an extreme form of the doctrine of biblical inerrancy, which insists that the Bible is perfect and without error, that it is complete, and that it answers all theological questions with clarity. With such perfection in the Bible, inerrantists argue, any further scriptural revelation would be superfluous and redundant. Often Latter-day Saints are confronted with some version of the following inerrantist logic:

1. All religious truth is found in the Bible.
2. The revelations of Joseph Smith are not found in the Bible.
3. Therefore the revelations of Joseph Smith are not religious truth.

But to this I would add the following:

4. Premise number 1 is not found in the Bible, either.

5. Therefore premise number 1 is not religious truth.
6. And if premise number 1 is not religious truth, then neither is conclusion 3, which is based upon it.

Extreme inerrantists will hotly dispute premise number 4; nevertheless it is true. There is not a single passage in the Bible that mentions the Bible—*Bible* is not a biblical word.

The greatest weakness of the extreme inerrantist position is that it accepts as its fundamental working principles propositions which are not themselves found in the Bible—for example, "the Bible is sufficient for salvation," "the Bible is inerrant," "the Bible answers all our religious questions," "the Bible gives us authority to speak and act for God," or "there will never be any more scriptures from God than the Bible." None of these propositions are themselves biblical, yet they are accepted as fundamental religious principles by people who claim to reject all nonbiblical religious principles.

The passage appealed to most often by extreme inerrantists is 2 Timothy 3:16–17: "All scripture is given by inspiration of God, and is profitable for doctrine, for reproof, for correction, for instruction in righteousness: that the man of God may be perfect, throughly furnished unto all good works." But this passage, as used by the inerrantists for their claims, merely begs the question, for it does not mention the Bible or describe what books should be in the Bible; it merely states that "all *scripture*" is "profitable." Indeed the Latter-day Saints would agree heartily that *all* scripture is profitable, including the Book of Mormon, the Doctrine and Covenants, and the Pearl of Great Price. The passage in 2 Timothy offers no criteria for determining what the canon of scripture ought to include. And even if it did, it does not say that the canon is closed or that the canon of scripture is sufficient, inerrant, or incapable of improvement; it merely states that all scripture is *profitable*. If I want to drive my car, it is *profitable* to have the keys, but just having the car keys is not enough if there is no gas in the tank or air in the tires. A thing can be profitable, or even necessary, without being sufficient. Paul's statement to Timothy clearly teaches that the man of God cannot be perfect without the scriptures, but it does not say that the scriptures alone make him perfect.[5] Any religious propositions as important as "all religious truth is found in the Bible," or "the Bible alone is sufficient," or "there can never be additions to the Bible," to be self-consistent, ought to be set forth in the Bible in clear, unmistakable terms, yet they are entirely missing.

Now, some conservative Protestants would argue that if Latter-day Saints don't accept this extreme form of biblical inerrancy, then by definition we are not Christians. But there are many Christians in the world—most, in fact—who do not believe that the Bible alone is sufficient for salvation, or that it is absolutely and literally perfect in every word, or that it answers every possible religious question with clarity. If all of these people—virtually every Christian in history except modern, conservative Protestants—are excluded from being Christians because they deny the extreme form of the doctrine of inerrancy, then the exclusion is nothing more than the religious imperialism of a sectarian minority and another example of a special definition for *Christian* (see chapter 1 herein). On the other hand, if Catholics, Orthodox, and mainline Protestants are not excluded for rejecting this type of inerrancy, but Latter-day Saints are, then we are clearly dealing with a theological double standard.

Which Is the "Christian" Bible?

The real Achilles' heel of the canonical exclusion, however, lies elsewhere. It lies in the idea that there is one single Christian canon or one single Christian Bible, for historically there has not been one Christian canon or one Christian Bible, but many. For example, just before A.D. 200 someone in the Christian church at Rome wrote a list of the books that were accepted as canonical by the Roman church at that time. A copy of this canon list was discovered in 1740 by Lodovico Muratori in the Ambrosian Library in Milan, and for this reason it is called the Muratorian Canon.[6] According to it, the Roman church at the end of the second century did not consider Hebrews, James, 1 Peter, or 2 Peter to be scripture, and they accepted only two of the letters of John, although we cannot be sure which two. They did accept as canonical, however, two works now considered to be outside the New Testament, the Apocalypse of Peter and the Wisdom of Solomon. Clearly their canon of scripture was different from that of modern Christians, but does that mean that the second- and third-century Roman church was not Christian? Remember that these were the same people who were dying in the arenas for the sake of Christ. Can anyone seriously argue that they weren't Christians just because their canon was different?

The famous church historian Eusebius of Caesarea, writing about A.D. 300, proposed another canon.[7] He listed only twenty-one books as "recognized," and listed Hebrews, James, 2 Peter, 2 and 3 John, Jude, and Revelation as questionable or spurious.[8] Was the "Father of Church History" not a Christian? After all, his canon, his Bible, was not the modern "Christian" Bible. As Bruce M. Metzger summarizes, "The Eastern Church, as reported by Eusebius about A.D. 325, was in considerable doubt concerning the authority of most of the Catholic Epistles as well as the Apocalypse."[9]

Saint Gregory of Nazianzus rejected the book of Revelation in his fourth-century canon list, which was ratified three centuries later in 692 by the Trullan Synod. Even though Revelation was not included on his list, Gregory insisted, "You have all. If there is any besides these, it is not among the genuine [books]."[10] Were both the saint and the synod non-Christian because they deleted Revelation from the "Christian" Bible?

One of the most important of the Greek New Testament manuscripts, known as D or Codex Claromontanus, contains a canon list for both the Old and New Testaments. The manuscript itself is a product of the sixth century, but most scholars believe the canon list originated in the Alexandrian church in the fourth century.[11] This canon omits Philippians, 1 and 2 Thessalonians, and Hebrews, but includes the Epistle of Barnabas, the Shepherd of Hermas, the Acts of Paul (not our Acts), and, like the Muratorian Canon, the Apocalypse of Peter.

The first indication of a canon like that of modern Christians does not come until well into the fourth century, when Saint Athanasius, the bishop of Alexandria, recommended a list of acceptable books to his churches in his *Thirty-ninth Festal Letter* (A.D. 367). But Athanasius' canon did not become official until over a thousand years afterward.

Before the fifth century the Syrian Christian canon included 3 Corinthians and Tatian's Diatessaron, but excluded the four Gospels, Philemon, the seven general Epistles, and the book of Revelation. Syrian Christians from the fifth century on accepted the Syriac Peshitta version of the Bible, which included the four Gospels in place of the Diatessaron and excluded 3 Corinthians, but recognized only twenty-two books in all as canonical: the four Gospels, the book of Acts, the fourteen letters of Paul, James, 1 Peter, and 1 John. To this day both the Syrian Orthodox church and the Chaldean Syrian church recognize only these twenty-two books, rejecting 2 Peter, 2 and 3 John, Jude, and the book of Revelation.[12] It is also interesting to note that the Greek Orthodox church has never included the book of Revelation in its official lectionary.[13]

The Georgian and Armenian churches followed the Syrian churches in not accepting the book of Revelation until the tenth and twelfth centuries, respectively. The Abyssinian Orthodox church has in its canon the twenty-seven books of the modern New Testament, but adds the Synodos and Qalementos (both attributed to Clement of Rome), the Book of the Covenant (which includes a post-resurrection discourse of the Savior), and the Ethiopic Didascalia. To the Old Testament the Abyssinian canon adds the book of Enoch (cited as prophetic by the canonical book of Jude) and the Ascension of Isaiah.

The point of all this is not to suggest that any of the New Testament books are spurious, for Latter-day Saints accept all twenty-seven books of the New Testament. It is merely to show that there have been and still are Christians who differ from one another on the issue of canon and yet remain Christians. The idea that there is a single, fixed canon accepted by all Christians from the beginning of the Christian church is a myth. In fact the canon of scripture was not finally fixed authoritatively for Roman Catholics until 1546 at the Council of Trent. For most Protestant denominations the canon was officially fixed even later than this.[14]

Among Protestants, Martin Luther suggested that the New Testament books were of varying worth and divided them up into three separate ranks. In the prefaces of his early editions of the New Testament, Luther denied that the lowest rank (Hebrews, James, Jude, and Revelation) belonged among "the true and noblest books of the New Testament," and went so far as to call the Epistle of James "a letter of straw." He complained that Hebrews contradicted Paul by teaching that there was no repentance after baptism; that James contradicted Paul in teaching justification by works; that Jude merely copied from 2 Peter and from apocryphal books; and that Revelation dealt with material inappropriate for an Apostle, it didn't teach enough about Christ, and its author had too high an opinion of himself.[15] As a direct result of Luther's judgment, some subsequent Lutheran editions of the Bible separated Hebrews, James, Jude, and Revelation from the rest of the New Testament, and even went so far as to label them "apocryphal" and "noncanonical." As Bruce Metzger points out: "Thus we have a threefold division of the New Testament: 'Gospels and Acts', 'Epistles and Holy Apostles', and 'Apocryphal New Testament'—an arrangement that persisted for nearly a century in half a dozen or more printings."[16]

John Oecolampadius, the Reformation preacher at Basle, wrote in 1536 that "we do not consider the [book of] Revelation, together with the Epistles of James and Jude, and 2 Peter, and the last two Epistles of John, to be on a par with the rest [of the New Testament]."[17]

Once again let me say that the point of all this data is not to attack the modern Christian canon, but merely to show that many Christians—both Catholic and Protestant, both ancient and modern—have disagreed over what belonged in the canon and what did not. To allow them to diverge from a single, monolithic canon and remain Christians while calling Latter-day Saints non-Christians for doing the same thing is logically inconsistent, and constitutes another example of the theological double standard.

The Catholic Bible vs. the Protestant Bible

Finally, it should be understood that there is *still* no single Christian canon or Bible, for Protestants and Catholics disagree on whether the "deuterocanonical books" (what Protestants call the Apocrypha) are scripture. At the Council of Trent in 1546, Roman Catholics officially adopted a canon of scripture that included the Apocrypha as fully inspired and fully the word of God. Consequently these twelve books are found in modern Catholic editions of the Bible. The collection of books includes Tobit, Judith, the Wisdom of Solomon, Ecclesiasticus or Ben Sirach, Baruch, the Letter of Jeremiah, 1 Maccabees, 2 Maccabees, additions to Esther, and additions to Daniel (comprised of the Prayer of Azariah and the Song of the Three Young Men, Susanna and the Elders, and Bel and the Dragon).

These books were part of the Greek translation of the Old Testament known as the Septuagint, which was in use in Egypt as early as the second century B.C. The Septuagint was also the version of the Old Testament used by the early Christian church, and so had passed into the Latin Vulgate of the Roman church, and is still the version used by the Greek Orthodox. The conciliar decree *De Canonicis Scripturis*, issued on 8 April 1546, declared that all who did not accept these deuterocanonical books (the Apocrypha) as Christian scripture were anathema (accursed).

On the other hand, most Protestants broke with the centuries-old tradition of accepting the Septuagint and all its contents, and preferred the version of the Old Testament which had been preserved in Hebrew by the Jews. These medieval copies of the Hebrew Old Testament did not have the Apocrypha in them as the Greek Septuagint translation did, and consequently the books of the Apocrypha are not generally accepted as scripture by Protestants. Thus the Roman Catholic and Greek Orthodox Bible is around twelve books, or approximately 230 pages, longer than the usual Protestant Bible, and for this canonical shortcoming Protestants fall under the anathema of the Council of Trent. Yet Protestants and Catholics continue to call each other Christians, even though one or the other of them has added to or deleted from the "Christian" canon. If the Catholics and Orthodox can have twelve more books in their Bibles than Protestants do and still be considered Christians, then why can't Mormons add the Book of Mormon, the Doctrine and Covenants, and the Pearl of Great Price? What's fair for one is fair for all.

In fact, in the interests of Christian unity Protestants and Catholics have "agreed to disagree" among themselves on the issue of canon. Each party feels that it is right and that the other is wrong; but they both feel that the issue of whose canon is correct is not serious enough to justify calling one another "non-Christian." This is why it is so unfair when this same issue is raised against the Latter-day Saints. If there is a single Christian canon and a single Christian Bible which Mormons must adopt in order to be Christians, then which one is it? Is the "Christian" Bible the one published by Catholics or the one published by Protestants? And if Protestants and Catholics cannot agree on this issue, yet *both* remain Christian, then how can the issue consistently be used to exclude Mormons from the family of Christian churches? This is to apply an exclusion to the Latter-day Saints that the other churches do not apply among themselves.

Summary

It is true that the Latter-day Saints have an expanded canon of scripture. But the Christian canon of scripture was not closed either by biblical or apostolic declaration, nor were its contents fixed or agreed upon in the apostolic period. The perception that the canon was closed grew up in later periods, though no single canon of scripture, or even of the New Testament books, has ever been agreed to by all Christian denominations. When revelation ceased after the death of the Apostles, the church was forced to draw one of two conclusions: Either revelation had ceased because God had said everything he wanted to say, and the church didn't need any more revelation; or revelation had ceased be-

cause there were no more Apostles and prophets to receive it,
and the church was lacking one of its necessary components.
Traditional Christians accept the former explanation; Latter-day
Saints accept the latter.

The Bible as we know it in the modern period is a product of
the Christian church, rather than the other way around. Since it
is clear that there were Christians before the New Testament was
written, it cannot be maintained that the Bible is what makes one
a Christian. Latter-day Saints reject this and all other enthusiastic
claims *about* the Bible that cannot be found *in* the Bible.

To this day Christians disagree on which books are the word
of God—that is, which books belong in a "Christian" Bible. During the Christian era there has been a variety of disagreements
over which books should be part of the New Testament canon.
Moreover, Catholics have added (or have Protestants deleted?) a
large collection of books found in the ancient Greek manuscripts
of the early Christian church and used by some Christians for
centuries. The truth is that traditional Christendom has never
been unanimous on the issues of canon and the Bible. If the
modern churches can strongly disagree among themselves as to
what the canon of Christian scripture is, and yet continue to accept each other as Christians, then it is logically inconsistent and
manifestly unfair to deny the Latter-day Saints the same privilege.

6

The Doctrinal Exclusion

The exclusion used most often to declare Latter-day Saints non-Christian is the doctrinal exclusion. The many forms this exclusion takes can really be reduced to the same logical argument: Since the Latter-day Saints do not believe what other Christians believe, they must not be Christians. A general weakness of this type of argument is the faulty assumption that all other Christians believe "what Christians believe." By this I mean that no two denominations, and few individual Christians, agree on every detail of Christian doctrine. Most denominations don't even agree on which doctrines are central and must be affirmed by all Christians, and which ones are peripheral and open to debate. Doctrinal diversity is simply a fact of life among the various Christian churches, so how can it be fair to demand of the Latter-day Saints that they alone manifest no doctrinal diversity? And what is the standard or norm by which such "doctrinal diversity" is to be measured? Even if such a demand were fair, it would still be impossible to comply with it, for there is no single, monolithic body of doctrine accepted by all Christians with which the Latter-day Saints could agree, even if they wanted to. Though many Christians have insisted that there *is* such a universal standard, so far no one has been able to define it to the satisfaction of all the others.

Which Is the "Christian" Doctrine?

Suppose for a moment that the Latter-day Saints were to take seriously the demand that they conform in every particular to "Christian" doctrine, and that they then made the attempt to do so. Having complied with such a demand, would the Latter-day Saints find themselves in total agreement with Protestants or with Catholics? Would they believe in apostolic succession or in the priesthood of all believers? Would they recognize an archbishop, a patriarch, a pope, a monarch, or no one at all as the head of Christ's church on earth? Would they be saved by grace alone, or would they find the sacraments of the church necessary for salvation? Would they believe in free will or in predestination? Would they practice water baptism? If so, would it be by immersion, sprinkling, or some other method? Would they believe in a substitutionary, representative, or exemplary atonement? Would they or would they not believe in "original sin"? And on and on.

It is unreasonable for other Christians to demand that Latter-day Saints conform to a single standard of "Christian" doctrine when they do not agree among themselves upon exactly what that standard is. To do so is to establish a double standard; doctrinal diversity is tolerated in some churches, but not in others. The often-heard claim that all true Christians share a common core of necessary Christian doctrine rests on the dubious proposition that all present differences between Christian denominations are over purely secondary or even trivial matters — matters not central to Christian faith. This view is very difficult to defend in the light of Christian history, and might be easier to accept if Protestants and Catholics — or Protestants and Protestants, for that matter — had not once burned each other at the stake as non-Christian heretics over these same "trivial" differences.

Is Christian Doctrine Always Biblical?

Often those who apply the doctrinal exclusion confuse the terms *Christian doctrine* and *biblical doctrine.* Many Christian denominations believe and teach things for doctrine that are not found in the Bible. For example, some Protestants believe that dancing is a sin. Catholics believe in the immaculate conception of Mary. Both Protestants and Catholics believe the doctrinal pronouncements of at least some of the ecumenical councils, yet *all* such pronouncements are extrabiblical. The Nicene Creed insists that the Father and the Son are *consubstantial* (Greek *homoousios*), but neither the word nor the concept is biblical. Yet the Nicene Creed must certainly be considered Christian in the sense that it was written by Christians to help define their beliefs about Christ. Its doctrine is Christian in the generic sense, even though it is not actually biblical in its content.

Is Christian Doctrine Always True?

Those who employ the doctrinal exclusion also frequently confuse the issue of whether a doctrine is true with whether belief in that doctrine necessarily renders one a non-Christian. They confuse being Christian with being correct. Often the doctrinal excluder perceives only two categories of believers: "those who believe what I believe," and "those who are not really Christians." And yet a logical necessity of having a family of Christian denominations is that one Christian may believe things other Christians don't, and still be considered a Christian. Thus, despite the doctrinal excluder's dichotomized view of things, there must be a third category of believers—true Christians whose beliefs differ from one's own.

Critics of the Latter-day Saints frequently assume that if this or that LDS belief can be proved incorrect, it proves that Latter-day Saints aren't Christians. But the two issues (being correct and being Christian) are logically separate. Many Christian denominations hold views that are believed false by other Christian denominations. For example, Catholics believe in the Assumption of the Virgin and in her role as a mediatrix in heaven, while Protestants do not. Protestants generally believe that the Bible is sufficient for salvation, while Catholics do not. Surely these issues are doctrinally significant, and just as surely either Protestants or Catholics must be mistaken about them. Yet neither side (not counting ultraconservatives) insists that the other is non-Christian merely because of its beliefs on these issues. While there is no way to prove the doctrines either true or false, they must be one or the other. And one side or the other will turn out to be wrong. Each feels very strongly that the other is wrong, but in the meantime the denominations involved have agreed to disagree, and both sides of the question are tolerated as generically Christian points of view.

But if doctrinal diversity does not exclude from the Christian family those who disagree on these matters, how can it validly be applied to exclude the Latter-day Saints for disagreeing on others? If doctrinal variance is going to be tolerated in some degree between the older denominations, then in all fairness it cannot be used to selectively exclude the Latter-day Saints.

On the other hand, it has been argued that the diversity tolerated among other Christian denominations is a matter of flexibility within certain broad limits, and that some LDS doctrines are so foreign to either the New Testament or traditional Christianity that they violate even these broad limits and cannot therefore be tolerated. A close examination of the individual LDS doctrines most maligned by the critics on these grounds, however, produces some surprising results. Let's start with the issue that has received the most recent attention, the charge that the Latter-day Saints are pagan "god makers."

The Doctrine of Deification

It is indisputable that Latter-day Saints believe that God was once a human being and that human beings can become gods. The famous couplet of Lorenzo Snow, fifth President of the LDS church, states:

> As man now is, God once was;
> As God now is, man may be.[1]

It has been claimed by some that this is an altogether pagan doctrine that blasphemes the majesty of God. Not all Christians have thought so, however. In the second century Saint Irenaeus, the most important Christian theologian of his time, said much the same thing as Lorenzo Snow:

> If the Word became a man,
> It was so men may become gods.[2]

Indeed, Saint Irenaeus had more than this to say on the subject of deification:

> Do we cast blame on him [God] because we were not made gods from the beginning, but were at first created merely as men, and then later as gods? Although God has

adopted this course out of his pure benevolence, that no one may charge him with discrimination or stinginess, he declares, "I have said, Ye are gods; and all of you are sons of the Most High." . . . For it was necessary at first that nature be exhibited, then after that what was mortal would be conquered and swallowed up in immortality.[3]

Also in the second century, Saint Clement of Alexandria wrote, "Yea, I say, the Word of God became a man so that you might learn from a man how to become a god"[4]—almost a paraphrase of Lorenzo Snow's statement. Clement also said that "if one knows himself, he will know God, and knowing God will become like God. . . . His is beauty, true beauty, for it is God, and that man becomes a god, since God wills it. So Heraclitus was right when he said, 'Men are gods, and gods are men.' "[5]

Still in the second century, Saint Justin Martyr insisted that in the beginning men "were made like God, free from suffering and death," and that they are thus "deemed worthy of becoming gods and of having power to become sons of the highest."[6]

In the early fourth century Saint Athanasius—that tireless foe of heresy after whom the orthodox Athanasian Creed is named—also stated his belief in deification in terms very similar to those of Lorenzo Snow: "The Word was made flesh in order that we might be enabled to be made gods. . . . Just as the Lord, putting on the body, became a man, so also we men are both deified through his flesh, and henceforth inherit everlasting life."[7] On another occasion Athanasius stated, "He became man that we might be made divine"[8]—yet another parallel to Lorenzo Snow's expression.

Finally, Saint Augustine himself, the greatest of the Christian Fathers, said: "But he himself that justifies also deifies, for by justifying he makes sons of God. 'For he has given them power to become the sons of God' [John 1:12]. If then we have been made sons of God, we have also been made gods."[9]

Notice that I am citing only unimpeachable Christian authorities here—no pagans, no Gnostics. All five of the above writers were not just Christians, and not just orthodox Christians —they were orthodox Christian *saints*. Three of the five wrote within a hundred years of the period of the Apostles, and all five believed in the doctrine of deification. This doctrine was a part of historical Christianity until relatively recent times, and it is still an important doctrine in some Eastern Orthodox churches. Those who accuse the Latter-day Saints of making up the doctrine simply do not know the history of Christian doctrine. In one of the best works on Catholicism, Father Richard P. McBrien states that a fundamental principle of orthodoxy in the patristic period was to see "the history of the universe as *the history of divinization and salvation*." As a result the Fathers concluded, according to McBrien, that "because the Spirit is truly God, we are truly *divinized* by the presence of the Spirit."[10]

In *The Westminster Dictionary of Christian Theology*, which is not a Mormon publication, the following additional information can be found in the article titled, "Deification":

> Deification (Greek *theosis*) is for Orthodoxy the goal of every Christian. Man, according to the Bible, is 'made in the image and likeness of God'. . . . It is possible for man to become like God, to become deified, to become god by grace. This doctrine is based on many passages of both OT and NT (e.g. Ps. 82 (81).6; II Peter 1.4), and it is essentially the teaching both of St Paul, though he tends to use the language of filial adoption (cf. Rom. 8.9–17; Gal. 4.5–7), and the Fourth Gospel (cf. 17.21–23).
>
> The language of II Peter is taken up by St Irenaeus, in his famous phrase, 'if the Word has been made man, it is so that men may be made gods' (*Adv. Haer* V, Pref.), and becomes the standard in Greek theology. In the fourth century St Athanasius repeats Irenaeus almost word for word, and in the fifth century St Cyril of Alexandria says that we shall become sons 'by participation' (Greek *methexis*). Deification is the central idea in the spirituality of St Maximus the Confessor, for whom the doctrine is the corollary of the Incarnation: 'Deification, briefly, is the encompassing and fulfilment of all times and ages', . . . and St Symeon the New Theologian at the end of the tenth century writes, 'He who is God by nature converses with those whom he has made gods by grace, as a friend converses with his friends, face to face.' . . .
>
> Finally, it should be noted that deification does not mean absorption into God, since the deified creature remains itself and distinct. It is the whole human being, body and soul, who is transfigured in the Spirit into the likeness of the divine nature, and deification is the goal of every Christian.[11]

Whether the doctrine of deification is correct or incorrect, it was a part of mainstream Christian orthodoxy for centuries, though some modern Christians with a limited historical view may not be aware of it. If this doctrine became "the standard in Greek theology," and if "deification is the goal of every Christian," then the Latter-day Saints can't be banished from the Christian family for having the same theology and the same goal. If Saint Irenaeus, Saint Justin Martyr, Saint Clement of Alexandria, Saint Athanasius, Saint Cyril of Alexandria, Saint Maximus the Confessor, and Saint Symeon the New Theologian all believed that human beings can become gods, and if these good former-day saints are still to be counted as Christians, then the Latter-day Saints cannot be excluded from Christian circles for believing the same thing. In fact this doctrine is not pagan, nor is it foreign to the larger Christian tradition.[12] Since it is found among the theologian/saints from Justin Martyr in the second century to Simeon the New Theologian in the eleventh century, Joseph Smith obviously did not make it up.

There is often much more to the history of Christianity and of Christian doctrine than just what seems familiar and comfortable to twentieth-century conservatives. Yet even among conservative Protestants the doctrine of deification is still occasionally found. Paul Crouch of the Trinity Broadcasting Network says: "I am a little god. I have His name. I am one with Him. I'm in covenant relation. I am a little god. Critics begone."[13] Robert Tilton, a Texas evangelist, says that man is " a God kind of creature. Originally you were designed to be as a god in this world. Man was designed or created by God to be the god of this world."[14] Kenneth Copeland, also of Texas, tells his listeners, "You don't have a god in you. You are one!"[15] He writes that "man had total authority to rule as a god over every living creature on earth."[16]

Now, in fact, the Latter-day Saints would not agree with the doctrine of deification as understood by most of these evangelists, for in the LDS view we receive the full divine inheritance only through the atonement of Christ and only after a glorious resurrection. Closer to the Latter-day Saint understanding of the doctrine are the views expressed by C. S. Lewis, an individual whose genuine Christianity is virtually undisputed: "It is a serious thing to live in a society of possible gods and goddesses, to remember that the dullest and most uninteresting person you can talk to may one day be a creature which, if you sa[w] it now, you would be strongly tempted to worship."[17]

Elsewhere Lewis writes that the great promise of Christianity is that humans can share Christ's type of life (Greek *zoe* rather than *bios*) and thus can become sons and daughters of God. He explains: "[Christ] came to this world and became a man in order to spread to other men the kind of life He has—by what I call 'good infection.' Every Christian is to become a little Christ."[18] In words reminiscent of those used by the Christian Fathers as well as Lorenzo Snow, Lewis succinctly states: "The Son of God became a man to enable men to become sons of God."[19]

In a fuller statement of his doctrine of deification, Lewis practically states the LDS view:

> The command *Be ye perfect* is not idealistic gas. Nor is it a command to do the impossible. He is going to make us into creatures that can obey that command. He said (in the Bible) that we were "gods" and He is going to make good His words. If we let Him—for we can prevent Him, if we choose—He will make the feeblest and filthiest of us into a god or goddess, dazzling, radiant, immortal creature, pulsating all through with such energy and joy and wisdom and love as we cannot now imagine, a bright stainless mirror which reflects back to God perfectly (though, of course, on a smaller scale) His own boundless power and delight and goodness. The process will be long and in parts very painful; but that is what we are in for. Nothing less. He meant what He said.[20]

If C. S. Lewis can think of human beings as "possible gods and goddesses," if he can maintain that "He will make the feeblest and filthiest of us into a god or goddess," and if he is still to be considered a Christian—then how can the Latter-day Saints be excluded from the Christian family as rank pagans for believing exactly the same things?[21]

Critics of the Latter-day Saints may respond that the early Christian saints, the later Greek theologians, and C. S. Lewis all understand the doctrine of deification differently than the Latter-day Saints do, but this is untrue in the case of the early Christians and C. S. Lewis. Anyway, such a response amounts to a quibble, for it retreats abjectly from the claim that deification is a pagan doctrine wholly foreign to true Christianity. It argues instead that deification is a Christian doctrine misunderstood by the Latter-day Saints (and abandoned by most others, I might add). But if that is true, then the doctrinal exclusion is no longer valid when based on this doctrine, for—whether the Latter-day Saints interpret it "correctly" or not—deification is not a doctrine they made up out of thin air or borrowed from ancient paganism, nor is it totally foreign and repugnant to true Christianity, nor does it violate the broad limits of what has historically been considered Christian.

It should be noted here that the LDS doctrine of deification is often misrepresented. Despite what our critics claim, the Latter-day Saints do not believe that human beings will ever become the equals of God, or be independent of God, or that they will ever cease to be subordinate to God. For Latter-day Saints, to become gods means to overcome the world through the atonement of Christ (1 John 5:4–5; Revelation 2:7, 11). Thus we become heirs of God and joint-heirs with Christ (Romans 8:17; Galatians 4:7) and will inherit *all* things just as Christ inherits all things (1 Corinthians 3:21–23; Revelation 21:7). There are no limitations on these scriptural declarations; we shall inherit *all* things — including the power to create and to beget. In that glorified state we shall look like our Savior (1 John 3:2; 1 Corinthians 15:49; 2 Corinthians 3:18); we shall receive his glory and be one with him and with the Father (John 17:21–23; Philippians 3:21). Sitting with God upon the throne of God, we shall rule over all things (Luke 12:44; Revelation 3:21).

Now, if the Christian scriptures teach that we will look like God, receive the inheritance of God, receive the glory of God, be one with God, sit upon the throne of God, and exercise the power and rule of God, then surely it cannot be un-Christian to conclude with C. S. Lewis and others that such beings as these can be *called* gods, as long as we remember that this use of the term *gods* does not in any way reduce or limit the sovereignty of God our Father. That is how the early Christians used the term; it is how C. S. Lewis used the term; and it is how the Latter-day Saints use the term and understand the doctrine.

The Plurality of Gods

Actually the real objection in modern Christian churches to the doctrine of deification is often that it implies the existence of more than one God. If human beings can become gods and yet remain distinct beings separate from God, it makes for a universe with many gods. Surely C. S. Lewis realized this implication; so did the early Christian saints. Yet like the Latter-day Saints they did not understand this implication to constitute genuine polytheism.

For both the doctrine of deification and the implied doctrine of plurality of gods, an understanding of the definitions involved is essential. So let's be clear on what Latter-day Saints do *not* believe. They do not believe that humans will ever be equal to or independent of God. His status in relation to us is not in any way compromised. There is only one source of light, knowledge, and power in the universe. If through the gospel of Jesus Christ and the grace of God we receive the fulness of God (Ephesians 3:19) so that we also can be called gods, humans will never become "ultimate" beings in the abstract, philosophical sense. That is, even as they sit on thrones exercising the powers of gods, those who have become gods by grace remain eternally subordinate to the source of that grace; they are extensions of their Father's power and agents of his will. They will continue to worship and serve the Father, the Son, and the Holy Ghost forever, and will worship and serve no one and nothing else.

If the Latter-day Saints had chosen to refer to such glorified beings as "angels" instead of "gods," it is unlikely anyone outside the LDS church would have objected to the doctrine per se. It seems that it is only the *term* that is objectionable. And yet the scriptures themselves often use the word *god* in this limited sense to refer to nonultimate beings.

For example, in Psalm 8 the word *gods* (Hebrew *elohim*) is used in reference to the angels: "What is man, that thou art mindful of him? and the son of man, that thou visitest him? For thou hast made him a little lower than the angels [*elohim*], and hast crowned him with glory and honour." (Vv. 4–5.) Though the Hebrew reads "gods" (*elohim*), translators and commentators from the Septuagint on, including the author of Hebrews in the New Testament, have understood the expression to refer to the angels (see Hebrews 2:7). The term *gods* is here applied to beings other than God. Deuteronomy 10:17, Joshua 22:22, and Psalm 136:2 all insist that God is a "God of gods." Clearly this doesn't mean that there are divine competitors out in the cosmos somewhere; rather, these passages probably also refer to the angels in their divinely appointed roles. If the angels can, in some sense, be considered divine beings because they exercise the powers of God and act as his agents, then the one God they serve is correctly considered a "God of gods." Scholars have long known, and the Dead Sea Scrolls and other literature of the period have now proven, that the Jews in Jesus' day commonly referred to the angels as "gods" (Hebrew *elim* or *elohim*) in this nonultimate sense.[22] This is not because the Jews were polytheists, but because they used the term *god* in a limited sense to refer to other beings associated with God whom he allowed the privilege of exercising divine powers.

But human beings are also called "gods" in scripture, probably for the same reasons that the angels are—they, as well as the angels, can exercise the powers of God and act as his agents. Thus Moses is designated a "god to Pharaoh" (Exodus 7:1). This doesn't mean that Moses had become an exalted or ultimate being, but only that he had been given divine powers and was authorized to represent God to Pharaoh, even to the point of speaking God's word in the first person. If the scriptures can refer to a mortal human being like Moses as a "god" in this sense, then surely immortal human beings who inherit the fulness of God's powers and authority in the resurrection can be understood to be "gods" in the same sense.

In Exodus 21:6 and 22:8–9 human judges are referred to in the Hebrew text as *elohim* ("gods"). In Psalm 45:6 the king is referred to as an *elohim*. Human leaders and judges are also referred to as "gods" in the following passage from the book of Psalms: "God standeth in the congregation of the mighty; he judgeth among the gods. . . . I have said, Ye are gods; and all of you are children of the most High. But ye shall die like men, and fall like one of the princes." (Psalm 82:1, 6–7.) Jewish and Christian biblical scholars alike have understood this passage as applying the term *gods* to human beings. According to James S. Ackerman, who is not a Mormon, "the overwhelming majority of commentators have interpreted this passage as referring to Israelite judges who were called 'gods' because they had the high responsibility of dispensing justice according to God's Law."[23]

In the New Testament, at John 10:34–36, we read that Jesus himself quoted Psalm 82:6 and interpreted the term *gods* as referring to human beings who had received the word of God: "Jesus answered them, Is it not written in your law, I said, Ye are gods? If he called them gods, unto whom the word of God came, and the scripture cannot be broken; say ye of him, whom the Father hath sanctified, and sent into the world, Thou blasphemest; because I said, I am the Son of God?" In other words, 'If the scriptures [Psalm 82] can refer to mortals who receive the word of God as "gods," then why get upset with me for merely saying I am the Son of God?' The Savior's argument was effective precisely because the scripture *does* use the term *gods* in this limited way to refer to human beings. According to J. A. Emerton, who is also not a Mormon, "most exegetes are agreed that the argument is intended to prove that men can, in certain circumstances, be called gods. . . . [Jesus] goes back to fundamental principles and argues, more generally, that the word 'god' can, in certain circumstances, be applied to beings other than God himself, to whom he has committed authority."[24]

And that, in a nutshell, is the LDS view. Whether in this life or the next, through Christ human beings can be given the powers of God and the authority of God. Those who receive this great inheritance can properly be called gods. They are not gods in the Greek philosophic sense of "ultimate beings," nor do they compete with God, the source of their inheritance, as objects of worship. They remain eternally his begotten sons and daughters — therefore, never equal to him nor independent of him. Orthodox theologians may argue that Latter-day Saints shouldn't use the term *gods* for nonultimate beings, but this is because the Latter-day Saints' use of the term violates Platonic rather than biblical definitions. Both in the scriptures and in earliest Christianity those who received the word of God were called gods.

I don't need to repeat here the views of Christian saints and theologians cited above on the doctrine of deification. But it should be noted that for them, as for the Latter-day Saints, the doctrine of deification implied a plurality of "gods" but not a plurality of Gods. That is, it did not imply polytheism. Saint Clement of Alexandria was surely both a monotheist and a Christian, and yet he believed that those who are perfected through the gospel of Christ "are called by the appellation of gods, being destined to sit on thrones with the other gods that have been first installed in their places by the Savior."[25] This is good LDS doctrine. If Clement, the Christian saint and theologian, could teach that human beings will be called gods and will sit on thrones with others who have been made gods by Jesus Christ, how in all fairness can Joseph Smith be declared a polytheist and a non-Christian for teaching the same thing?

In harmony with widely recognized scriptural and historical precedents, Latter-day Saints use the term *gods* to describe those who will, through the grace of God and the gospel of Jesus Christ, receive of God's fulness — of his divine powers and prerogatives — in the resurrection. Thus, for Latter-day Saints the question "Is there more than one god?" is not the same as "Is there more than one source of power or object of worship in the universe?" For Latter-day Saints, as for Saint Clement, the answer to the former is yes, but the answer to the latter is no. For Latter-day Saints the term *god* is a title which can be extended to those who receive the power and authority of God as promised to the faithful in the scriptures; but such an extension of that title does not challenge, limit, or infringe upon the ultimate and absolute position and authority of the Father, the Son, and the Holy Ghost.

When anti-Mormon critics interpret Exodus 7:1, Deuteronomy 10:17, Psalm 8:5 (in Hebrew), Psalm 45:6, Psalm 82:6, or John 10:34–36, they go to great lengths to clarify that these scriptures use the term *god* in a limited sense and that therefore they do not involve any polytheism—there may be more than one "god," but there is only one God. When they discuss Latter-day Saint writings that use the term *god* in the same sense, however, the critics seldom offer the same courtesy. Instead they disallow any limited sense in which the term *gods* can be used when that term occurs in LDS sources, thereby distorting and misinterpreting our doctrine, and then accuse us of being "polytheists" for speaking of "gods" in a sense for which there are valid scriptural and historical precedents.

Other Christian saints, theologians, and writers—both ancient and modern—have believed human beings can become "gods" but have not been accused of polytheism, because the "gods" in this sense were viewed as remaining forever subordinate to the Father, the Son, and the Holy Ghost. Since this is also the doctrine of the Latter-day Saints, they also ought to enjoy the same defense against the charge of polytheism. Since these other Christians and the Latter-day Saints share the same doctrine, they should share the same fate; either make polytheist heretics of the saints, theologians, and writers in question, or allow the Latter-day Saints to be considered worshippers of the one true God.

Summary

The doctrinal exclusion is invalid often on general principles because it demands doctrinal conformity to a standard that does not really exist, to a "pure" Christianity which cannot be agreed upon by all Christians. Therefore it is a moving target which changes from denomination to denomination; all parties demand that Latter-day Saints be more "orthodox," but each defines "orthodoxy" differently. The doctrinal exclusion assumes that Christianity is one monolithic point of view when in fact the multiplicity of Christian denominations witnesses that it is not. Those who employ the doctrinal exclusion often recognize only two categories: those whose doctrine agrees with their own and those who are "not Christians." But without a third category—that is, Christians whose doctrine is different than one's own but who are still Christians—the very idea of a family of independent Christian denominations is impossible.

Still, the claim is made that certain LDS doctrines are so bizarre, so totally foreign to biblical or historical Christianity, that they simply cannot be tolerated. In terms of the LDS doctrines most often criticized on these grounds, however—the doctrine of deification and its corollary, the plurality of gods—this claim does not hold up to historical scrutiny. Early Christian saints and theologians, later Greek Orthodoxy, modern Protestant evangelists, and even C. S. Lewis have all professed their belief in a doctrine of deification. The scriptures themselves talk of many "gods" and use the term *god* in a limited sense for beings other than the Father, the Son, or the Holy Ghost. If this language is to be tolerated in scripture and in ancient and modern orthodox Christians without cries of "polytheism!" then it must be similarly tolerated in the Latter-day Saints. If scripture can use the term *gods* for nonultimate beings, if the early Church could, if Christ himself could, then Latter-day Saints cannot conceivably be accused of being outside the Christian tradition for using the same term in the same way.

Again, I am not arguing that the doctrine is *true*, although I certainly believe it is. I am only arguing that other Christians of unimpeachable orthodoxy have believed in deification long before the Latter-day Saints came along, and that it has been accepted and tolerated in them as part of their genuine Christianity. Fair play demands the same treatment for the Latter-day Saints.

7

The Doctrinal Exclusion: Trinity and the Nature of God

It has been said that since Latter-day Saints do not accept the Christian doctrine of the Trinity, it follows that they cannot be considered Christians. Here again the heart of the argument lies in the definition of its terms. Specifically the logical problem with this argument is that non-LDS Christians usually define the term *trinity* ambiguously. They habitually, and most often unconsciously, equate the biblical teaching on the nature of the Godhead with the later philosophical statement formulated at the Council of Chalcedon in A.D. 451—the Nicene Creed.[1] But these two ways of perceiving God are simply not equivalent.

What Is the Trinity?

If by "the doctrine of the Trinity" one means the New Testament teaching that there is a Father, a Son, and a Holy Ghost, all three of whom are fully divine, then Latter-day Saints believe in the doctrine of the Trinity. It is as simple as that. The Latter-day Saints' first article of faith, written by Joseph Smith in 1842, states, "We believe in God, the Eternal Father, and in His Son, Jesus Christ, and in the Holy Ghost." Baptisms in the Church are performed "in the name of the Father, and of the Son, and of the Holy Ghost" (see D&C 20:73). The prayer of blessing on the sacrament of the Lord's Supper is addressed to God the Eternal Father in the name of his Son, Jesus Christ, to the end that those who partake may have his Spirit to be with them (see D&C 20:77–79). Latter-day Saints thoroughly agree with the biblical doctrine of the threefold nature of the Godhead and of the divinity of the Father, the Son, and the Holy Ghost.

However, if by "the doctrine of the Trinity" one means the doctrine formulated by the councils of Nicaea and Chalcedon and elaborated upon by subsequent theologians and councils—that God is three coequal persons in one substance or essence—then Latter-day Saints do not believe it. They do not believe it, because it is not biblical. Words central to the orthodox understanding of the Trinity—words like *coequal, consubstantial,* and *circumincession,* or the word *trinity* itself, for that matter—are not found in scripture.[2] The term *trinity* (Latin *trinitas*) was first used by Tertullian around the beginning of the third century A.D.[3] The Nicene and Chalcedonian Fathers tried to find scriptural terms for their new formulae but were unable to do so.

The scriptures themselves do not offer any explanation of how the threeness and the oneness of God are related. The biblical writers were singularly uninterested in that problem or in questions dealing with God's essence, his substance, or the philosophical definition of his nature. These later concerns are elaborations upon the biblical doctrine of God, elaborations formulated to answer in philosophically respectable terms the questions and objections of Hellenistic thinking concerning the primitive Christian doctrine.[4] Christian intellectuals of the fourth and fifth centuries felt that the biblical language was too unsophisticated and inadequate for this purpose, and so they attempted to supplement and improve it with their own best efforts.

Did the Councils Write Scripture?

The Latter-day Saints accept both the oneness and the threeness of God—both are biblical. They reject, however, the attempts of the postbiblical church to define, for the sake and in the language of the philosophers, how the oneness and the threeness of God are related—attempts which amounted to putting words in God's mouth. If a proposition is not already found in the Bible, by what authority—in the absence of Apostles and prophets—can it be imposed on the church as the word of God? How can mere theologians expand upon or correct the doctrine of the Apostles? Can theologians add to the scriptures? Yet when the Latter-day Saints reject the doctrines of Nicaea and Chalcedon, which are clearly additions to the biblical teaching, they are accused of rejecting the *scriptural* view of God. This is simply a misrepresentation, unless one defines the words of the councils as supplemental scripture. Latter-day Saints do not believe that the words of the councils constitute additional scripture, and therefore they refuse to let the Nicene tail wag the biblical dog.

It is absurdly contradictory to say on the one hand, as some critics of the Latter-day Saints do, that the Bible alone is sufficient for salvation (the doctrine of *sola scriptura*), and then to add that one must also believe the creeds *in addition* to the Bible in order to even be a Christian. Some may respond that the creeds and teachings of the councils are merely useful as historically accepted summaries of the biblical doctrines, but this is not a fair assessment. Anyone who has passed freshman English knows that a true summary cannot introduce concepts or information not found in the material being summarized. And there is no passage of scripture or combination of scriptures for which the doctrine of an abstract, absolute, transcendent, consubstantial, co-eternal unity in trinity existing unknowably and incomprehensibly without body, parts, or passions and outside space and time can be called a fair "summary." There is a vast difference between a summary and an elaboration.

Modern scholars know that the Nicene doctrine of the Trinity not only differs from but also introduces new concepts to the biblical view. One such scholar notes, "It is clearly impossible (if one accepts historical evidence as relevant at all) to escape the claim that the later formulations of dogma cannot be reached by a process of deductive logic from the original propositions and must contain an element of novelty."[5] Further on this same scholar concludes, "The emergence of the full trinitarian doctrine was not possible without significant modification of previously accepted ideas."[6]

Thus the Latter-day Saints simply prefer to do without such conciliar "summaries" and to stick to the scriptures themselves. The *un*summarized Bible is fine just as it is; bring forward any creed composed entirely of scriptural passages and the Latter-day Saints will heartily affirm every word.

The Trinity in the New Testament

It is a matter of record that the Nicene doctrine of the Trinity is a postbiblical development—it is simply not found in the New Testament. In one of the major Christian treatments of the doctrine of the Trinity, Jesuit scholar Edmund J. Fortman, having examined the various parts of the New Testament individually, notes that "there is no trinitarian doctrine in the Synoptics or Acts." He also observes that in the New Testament "nowhere do we find any trinitarian doctrine of three distinct subjects of divine life and activity in the same Godhead," and that "in John there is no trinitarian formula."[7] Concerning the letters of Paul, Fortman states:

> These passages give no doctrine of the Trinity, but they show that Paul linked together Father, Son, and Holy Spirit. They give no trinitarian formula . . . but they offer material for the later development of trinitarian doctrine. . . . [Paul] has no formal trinitarian doctrine and no clear-cut realization of a trinitarian problem, but he furnishes much material for the later development of a trinitarian doctrine.[8]

After examining all parts of the New Testament, Fortman concludes that the classical doctrine of the Trinity is not biblical:

> There is no formal doctrine of the Trinity in the New Testament writers, if this means an explicit teaching that in one God there are three co-equal divine persons. But the three are there, Father, Son, and Holy Spirit, and a triadic ground plan is there, and triadic formulas are there. . . . The Biblical witness to God, as we have seen, did not contain any formal or formulated doctrine of the Trinity, any explicit teaching that in one God there are three co-equal divine persons.[9]

Latter-day Saints couldn't agree more. Biblical theology, like LDS theology, affirms the threefold nature of the Godhead; but, also like LDS theology, biblical theology lacks any indication of a Nicene understanding. The scholarly consensus is further affirmed in *Harper's Bible Dictionary:* "The formal doctrine of the Trinity as it was defined by the great church councils of the fourth and fifth centuries is not to be found in the New Testament."[10]

In his sketch of Paul's theology J. Fitzmyer notes that the Apostle's views as stated in the biblical text are unclear and undeveloped from a post-Nicene point of view: "This double series of texts manifests Paul's lack of clarity in his conception of the relation of the Spirit to the Son. Paul shares with the OT a more fluid notion of personality than the later theological refinements of nature, substance, and person. His lack of clarity should be respected for what it is and be regarded only as the starting point of the later development."[11] In other words, from an orthodox perspective Paul didn't understand the nature of God as clearly as the theologians of the fourth century. If Paul's views had first been proposed after the Council of Nicaea, they would have been viewed as inadequate or even as defective. The Latter-day Saints prefer to think that Paul's conception of the nature of God is clearer and more authoritative than all the theologians and philosophers after him combined. After all, it was Paul that spoke with the risen Lord and was caught up to the third heaven, not the theologians (Acts 9:3–6; 2 Corinthians 12:2–4).

Furthermore, even orthodox writers and theologians now admit the difficulty of identifying the post-Nicene view as biblical:

> Trinitarian discussion, Roman Catholic as well as other, presents a somewhat unsteady silhouette.
>
> Two things have happened. There is the recognition on the part of exegetes and Biblical theologians, including a constantly growing number of Roman Catholics, that one should not speak of Trinitarianism in the New Testament without serious qualification. There is also the closely parallel recognition on the part of historians of dogma and systematic theologians that when one does speak of an unqualified Trinitarianism, one has moved from the period of Christian origins to, say, the last quadrant of the 4th century.[12]

The Trinity in Early Christian Writings

Other Christians besides the Latter-day Saints have perceived the nature of God in non-Nicene terms without being declared non-Christian. We saw above that by Nicene standards even the Apostle Paul is viewed as "lacking clarity" on the nature of God. In addition the Apostolic Fathers and the Greek Apologists of the second century, many of whom were Christian saints, also conceived of God in terms that were defective as judged by post-Nicene orthodoxy. According to Fortman, the classical doctrine of the Trinity wasn't a part of Christianity in the apostolic period or in the early second century, either. Speaking of the Apostolic Fathers, he writes, "There is in them, of course, no trinitarian doctrine and no awareness of a trinitarian problem."[13]

Other scholars, the best in the field, agree in almost the same words. In his work *Early Christian Doctrines,* J. N. D. Kelly writes of the second-century Apostolic Fathers, "Of a doctrine of the Trinity in the strict sense there is of course no sign, although the Church's triadic formula left its mark everywhere."[14] Elsewhere in this same work, Kelly states, "The Church had to wait for more than three hundred years for a final synthesis, for not until the Council of Constantinople (381) was the formula of one God existing in three coequal Persons formally ratified."[15]

Many of the Apologists were subordinationist in their doctrine of the Son and of the Holy Spirit. This means that they conceived of the Son and the Spirit not as coequal, coeternal and consubstantial, but as subordinate Gods, contingent Gods, or even as creatures of God whose divinity is dependent upon the Father. Even orthodox scholars admit this, though often gingerly and apologetically:

> Where the doctrine [of the Trinity] was elaborated, as e.g. in the writings of the Apologists, the language remained on the whole indefinite, and, from a later standpoint, was even partly unorthodox. Sometimes it was not free from a certain subordinationism.[16]

> It [subordinationism] is a characteristic tendency in much Christian teaching of the first three centuries, and is a marked feature of such otherwise orthodox Fathers as St. Justin and Origen.[17]

Johannes Quasten says of Saint Justin Martyr—who saw Christ as "a second God, second numerically but not in will"—that "Justin tends to subordinationism as far as the relation between the Logos and the Father is concerned."[18] Until Origen, the Apologists understood the Logos (Christ) to have become the Son only after his expression from the Father, contrary to the teaching of Nicaea, and they did not clearly distinguish between the Logos and the Holy Ghost.[19] In short, by strict Nicene standards, the earlier Christian Apologists were incorrect in their perception of God. Modern scholars and theologians are intensely defensive of these early writers, however, and insist that it is "grossly unfair" to judge the Apologists or question their orthodoxy on the basis of post-Nicene theology.[20] I agree; but I must also insist that if the Apostolic Fathers and the Greek Apologists can be hotly defended as genuine Christians, though they lack Nicene orthodoxy, then Nicene orthodoxy cannot at the same time be proposed as a necessary condition for genuine Christianity.

Furthermore, modern scholars have shown that the Nicene doctrine was not understood in "orthodox" terms even by the bishops that first drafted it. The interpretation of the language and the consequent perception of the Godhead in the minds of the Nicene Fathers were not exactly those of later orthodox theologians.[21] Even though Eusebius of Caesarea, the "Father of Church History," signed the Nicene document, he was a thorough subordinationist who maintained that "everyone must admit the Father is prior to and pre-exists the Son," and that the existence of the Son depended upon a specific premeditated act by the pre-existing Father.[22] This is not orthodox trinitarian doctrine. The same subordinationist doctrine in the theology of the Latter-day Saints is labelled "non-Christian" by orthodox critics, but let it be remembered that Eusebius the subordinationist was one of the bishops who attended the ancient council and signed the creed!

Now, please note that I am not resorting to heterodox writers —Gnostics, Marcionites, and so on—for evidence here. I am referring to only the mainstream writers of Christian orthodoxy— the New Testament writers, the Apostolic Fathers, the Greek Apologists, and the Nicene Fathers themselves—to provide examples of Christians whose doctrine of God was not that of later trinitarianism. If Latter-day Saints can be criticized for not *perceiving* the biblical God in the same terms as other Christians, then many early Christian writers, saints, and theologians must be criticized on the same grounds. It is just not historically correct that all true Christians have, from the beginning, perceived God in exactly the same trinitarian terms.

It is not my aim here to attempt a refutation of the Nicene doctrine of the Trinity. While Latter-day Saints do not believe it, they do not accuse those who do believe it of being non-Christian. The Nicene doctrine is one way in which the biblical data can be interpreted, though it is one with which the Latter-day Saints disagree.

But I don't need to disprove the Nicene view for the purposes of my argument. For if Jesus didn't teach the Nicene doctrine of the Trinity; if the New Testament writers didn't have any conception of it; if the Apostolic Fathers didn't know about it or even appreciate the problems associated with it; and if the formula itself wasn't even developed until the fourth century and, even then, those who signed it didn't understand it in completely orthodox terms; then one cannot maintain that the Nicene doctrine, as interpreted by modern trinitarians, is essential to true Christianity, unless of course one wants to say that there weren't any true Christians before the fourth century—including Jesus, his disciples, and the New Testament Church.

The Trinity Today

Even today the Nicene doctrine of the Trinity is not understood in exactly the same way by all orthodox Christians. Beginning in the eighth century and officially since the eleventh century, Roman Catholics and Protestants have added the Latin phrase *filioque* (and from the Son) to the original text of the "Nicene" Creed[23] at the point in which that document says that the Holy Spirit proceeds from the Father. Thus, in the Western churches the orthodox doctrine says that the Holy Ghost proceeds from the Father *and from the Son (filioque)*, like a torch being lit simultaneously by two other torches. But in the Eastern churches it is maintained that the Holy Spirit, like the Son, proceeds from the Father alone, as when one torch lights first a second and then a third.

The Eastern churches hotly reject the addition of the *filioque* clause to the Nicene Creed as an unauthorized distortion of the doctrine of the Trinity. Frank Gavin observes, ''No single difference between East and West has aroused so much bitterness on the part of Orthodox writers as has the matter of the *Filioque*.''[24] Theologians of the Eastern churches insist that the *filioque* introduces a false concept of the nature of God—even a false god— into Christianity: ''By the dogma of the *Filioque* [the Western Trinity] the God of the philosophers and savants is introduced into the place of the Living God. . . . By the dogma of the procession of the Holy Spirit from the Father alone [the Eastern Trinity], the God of the philosophers is forever banished from the Holy of Holies.''[25]

Because of this issue of the *filioque*, then, Eastern Christians and Western Christians have different concepts of the nature of the Trinity. This may seem like a small detail to nontheologians, but it is a dispute over the very nature of God, and it is serious enough to have separated the theologies of the East and West for nine hundred years.

Latter-day Saints believe in the biblical Father, Son, and Holy Ghost, but we are accused of being non-Christians because our concept of their nature differs from that of other Christians. The *filioque* dispute is also a dispute over God's nature. If the argument used to exclude Latter-day Saints holds, and all true Christians must share the same concept of the Trinity, then either the Eastern or the Western church, and more likely the latter,[26] is not truly Christian. On the other hand, if dissimilar conceptions of the Trinity are allowed to Christians on both sides of the *filioque* dispute, then the original argument is discredited—differing conceptions of the nature of the Trinity do not necessarily render individuals non-Christian.

Ultimately, being Christian is less a matter of perceiving God in the same Nicene or Chalcedonian terms as other Christians do, and more a matter of perceiving God in the same biblical terms as the first Christians did. Did the atonement of Christ save first-century Corinthians and Galatians, even though they did not conceive of God in Nicene terms? Of course it did. And if that is true, then the atonement of Christ can and will save faithful Latter-day Saints who accept the New Testament witness yet do not conceive of God in Nicene terms.

"God Is a Spirit"

The Latter-day Saint concept of God differs from that of Nicene orthodoxy in more than just the latter's trinitarian doctrine. The Latter-day Saints teach that God the Father is an anthropomorphic being—that is, that he has a tangible body: "The Father has a body of flesh and bones as tangible as man's; the Son also; but the Holy Ghost has not a body of flesh and bones, but is a personage of Spirit. Were it not so, the Holy Ghost could not dwell in us." (D&C 130:22.)

Some critics of the Latter-day Saints have argued that belief in an anthropomorphic Deity represents a departure not merely from the Nicene conception of God but from the biblical teaching as well, since John 4:24 teaches very clearly that "God is a Spirit: and they that worship him must worship him in spirit and in truth." But the Latter-day Saints do not dispute this passage at all, unless it is interpreted as limiting God to being *merely* a spirit.

For even trinitarians must interpret John 4:24 in a way that allows for the corporeality of the resurrected Christ. Two of the most fundamental teachings of the New Testament are that Christ is genuinely God and that he is at the same time genuinely corporeal, both in his incarnation and in his bodily resurrection. Since the trinitarian God must include the person of the Son — who is a physically resurrected being — the statement "God is a Spirit" cannot be understood, *even from a Nicene perspective*, as limiting God in all contexts to noncorporeality.

Actually John 4:24 should be translated "God is Spirit" rather than "God is *a* Spirit," for there is no indefinite article (*a, an*) in the Greek language, and it is always a matter of subjective judgment as to when the translator should add one. The consensus among biblical scholars is that there should *not* be an indefinite article at John 4:24. C. H. Dodd insists that "to translate [John 4:24] 'God is a Spirit' is the most gross perversion of the meaning."[27] According to Raymond E. Brown the passage at John 4:24

> is not an essential definition of God, but a description of God's dealing with men; it means that God is Spirit toward men because He gives the Spirit (xiv 16) which begets them anew. There are two other such descriptions in the Johannine writings: "God is light" (1 John i 5), and "God is love" (1 John iv 8). These too refer to the God who acts; God gives the world His Son, the *light* of the world (iii 19, viii 12, ix 5) as a sign of His *love* (iii 16).[28]

Just as God is not limited to being light and nothing else by 1 John 1:5, or to being love and nothing else by 1 John 4:8, so he is not limited to being spirit and nothing else by John 4:24 — unless one *assumes* with the Greeks that spirit and matter are mutually exclusive, opposing categories. That God *is* spirit does not limit him to being *a* spirit any more than his being worshipped *in* spirit (John 4:24) requires worshippers to first jettison their physical bodies.

Like first-century Jewish Christians, the Latter-day Saints do not understand the categories of "spirit" and "element" to be mutually exclusive. According to Joseph Smith, "there is no such thing as immaterial matter. All spirit is matter, but it is more fine or pure, and can only be discerned by purer eyes" (D&C 131:7). Thus Latter-day Saints understand the term *spiritual* to mean "infused with spirit," whereas Hellenized Christianity would understand it to mean "incorporeal." For the Latter-day Saints, being spiritual or being spirit does not imply being incorporeal. For example, D&C 93:33 indicates that even "man is spirit," though man is definitely corporeal as well.[29] Spirit and element are both compatible parts of the eternal whole. A strict mind/body or spirit/element dualism was foreign to Judaism and earliest Christianity until it was introduced by Hellenistic thinking. In the LDS view God *is* spirit, but he is not *merely* a spirit.

Latter-day Saints sometimes give the mistaken impression that because they believe the Father has a body "as tangible as man's," they believe him to be corporeal in the limited human sense. But this is not the case. God is spirit, but he is also element; both aspects of existence are included and encompassed within his glorious being. That he is either one does not limit the fact that he is also the other — and infinitely more.

God as a Spirit

Moreover, for the Latter-day Saints God most certainly *is* a spirit when manifest in the person of the Holy Ghost — "the Holy Ghost has not a body of flesh and bones, but is a personage of Spirit" (D&C 130:22). In the vast majority of cases, when human beings encounter or experience God, it is God manifest in the person of the Holy Ghost. This is the "gift" given to Christians in conversion and confirmation (Acts 2:38; 8:17; Luke 11:13). The Holy Ghost is both the Comforter and the Spirit of inspiration. It is undisputed both by LDS and non-LDS Christians that God is experienced as a spirit (the Holy Ghost) in most of the contexts in which human beings encounter him.

God as a Corporeal Being

Nevertheless, despite John 4:24 there are many other scriptures clearly teaching that, in the person of Jesus Christ, God also has a tangible body. This doctrine of the incarnation is common to Mormons and non-Mormons alike. After his resurrection, Jesus assured the Apostles that he was *not* merely a spirit: "Behold my hands and my feet, that it is I myself: handle me, and see; for a spirit hath not flesh and bones, as ye see me have" (Luke 24:39). The logic is not difficult: Jesus is God; Jesus has a body of flesh and bones; therefore, God, in the person of the resurrected Son, has a body of flesh and bones. Since both LDS Christians and orthodox Christians affirm the doctrines of the incarnation and bodily resurrection of God the Son, then in the person of the Son, God must be understood to have a tangible body.

Since God, or the Godhead, consists of three persons for Latter-day Saints and trinitarians alike, it does not seem to me any more outrageous or un-Christian to think of the Father as corporeal, as the Son is corporeal, than to think of him as a personage of spirit, like the Holy Ghost. Both Mormons and non-Mormons accept that "God is Spirit," but since the New Testament does not specify whether that means the Father has "a tangible body infused with spirit" or is "incorporeal" (both phraseologies are unbiblical), neither interpretation is more or less biblical or "Christian" than the other.

Nor can one argue, as Hellenized theology often did, that possession of a tangible body is somehow incompatible with divinity, for the Bible has already established both the tangible body (Luke 24:39) and the full divinity (John 1:1) of the resurrected Son. If God the Son can be fully divine and yet possess flesh and bones, there is no *a priori* reason why God the Father could not have a body also—unless, of course, one insists on strictly Platonic definitions of God.[30]

The God of the Philosophers

The real objection to the LDS belief in an anthropomorphic Father comes not from the Hebraic world of the first Christians, nor from Jesus and his Jewish disciples, nor from their Judeo-Christian writings. The real objections are rooted in the God of the philosophers, in the Hellenistic conception of God as an absolute being—abstract, ultimate, and transcendent. The LDS God is the God of the Hebrew Bible, but he is not the God of the philosophers. Regarding these two differing perceptions of God, Shaye J. D. Cohen observes:

> The God of the Hebrew Bible is very different from the supreme God of Plato or Aristotle. The former is an anthropomorphic being capable of anger, joy, and other emotions, who created the world and continues to direct human affairs. The God of the philosophers, however, was a much less human and much more abstract figure, incapable of emotion, and far removed from the daily concerns of humanity. Many Jews tried to combine these two conceptions, or, more precisely, to reinterpret the God of the Bible in the light of the ideas of the philosophers, espe-

cially Plato. . . . This approach to scripture was developed even further by Origen, Ambrose, and other fathers of the church.[31]

The God of the Nicene Council is, in a sense, a convert. He represents the God of the Hebrew scriptures converted into nonbiblical, philosophical terms. While the Nicene God was a divinity with whom the Hellenistic Christians of the fourth and fifth centuries could feel more intellectually comfortable than with the God described in the "primitive" language of the New Testament, he was no longer the God of first-century Jewish Christianity. Cohen continues:

> The God of the Hebrew Bible is for the most part an anthropomorphic and anthropopathic being, that is, a God who has the form and emotions of humans. . . . The God of the philosophers is a different sort of being altogether: abstract (the Prime Mover, the First Cause, the Mind or Soul of the Universe, etc.), immutable and relatively unconcerned with the affairs of humanity. . . . Popular piety does not need or want an immutable and shapeless Prime Mover; it wants a God who reveals himself to people, listens to prayer, and can be grasped in human terms. This is the God of the *Shema*, the Bible, and the liturgy. This is the God of practically all the Hebrew and Aramaic, and some of the Greek, Jewish literature of antiquity. It is not, however, the God of the philosophers.[32]

Nor is the concept of an anthropomorphic Deity so bizarre and foreign to Christianity that it must put the Latter-day Saints beyond the Christian pale. To cite but one example, as late as the fourth and fifth centuries most of the Christian monks of Egypt, relying on biblical passages for their concept of God the Father, believed him to have a human form. For this reason they are often referred to as "anthropomorphites." Following the Council of Constantinople in 381, however, such views were more frequently suppressed, and the new orthodoxy, in the face of considerable resistance, was imposed more stringently upon the holy monks of the desert monasteries. In 399, when a letter from Theophilus, the bishop of Alexandria, insisted that the biblical description of God was only allegorical and that the monks must not attribute to God any anthropomorphic characteristics, one Sarapion, an elderly monk of great reputation, found himself unable to pray to the new God, this God of the philosophers, at all. Falling on the ground he groaned: "Woe is me! They have taken my God away from me, and I have none to grasp, and I know not whom to adore or to address."[33] Ultimately the anthropomorphite monks simply rebelled and refused to accept the new view, successfully forcing their bishop Theophilus into an abrupt about-face.[34]

A God without Passions

In actual practice the vast majority of modern Christians, like the monk Sarapion, *conceive* of God in quite concrete and anthropomorphic terms. Despite the objections of theologians, Christians insist on praying to a loving Heavenly Father, "naively" conceived as anthropomorphic according to the biblical model. Yet, according to the strict orthodoxy of the councils and creeds, God is not really our Father in anything but an allegorical or adoptive sense; nor does he exist *in* heaven in the sense of having location;[35] nor does he love us in the sense of actually *feeling*, of being moved by any emotion. The philosophers who had gained control of Christian theology felt that if God could be located in any one place, then he was subject to the limit of location and was not absolute, and hence, according to Greek definitions, not God. The Greek God could not be subject to either time or space. Similarly the Greek ideal held that God must be *apatheia* (impassible), without passions or emotions. Otherwise, his will would be *subject* to his emotions and feelings, and in the Greek view God cannot be subject to anything. This is why the God of the philosophers must be not only without body but also without passions (feelings and emotions).[36] Van A. Harvey explains:

> Impassibility means not capable of being affected or acted upon and has been attributed to God alone in classical theism and Christian Orthodoxy. The presupposition of this attribution is *the Greek idea* that passibility involves potentiality, and potentiality, change. . . .
>
> Since Biblical and Hebraic thought is marked throughout by the conviction that God is a loving, compassionate being who acts, the attribution of [impassibility] has always constituted something of a problem for classical theologians.[37]

Augustine and others went to great lengths to insist that just as the corporeal references to God in the Bible must be reinterpreted in a noncorporeal way, so also all references to emotions in God must be interpreted in a nonemotive sense. For example, Augustine stated: "Now when God is said [in the Bible] to be angry, we do not attribute to him such a disturbed feeling as exists in the mind of an angry man; we merely refer to his just displeasure against sin by the term 'anger,' a word transferred by analogy from human emotions."[38] So in Augustine's mind God does not actually feel the emotion of anger. The big problem, of course, is that love is also an emotion, a passion, and the scriptures insist on the love of God ("God is love," "For God so loved the world," and so on). The philosophers got around this problem by simply redefining love whenever it was applied to God, so that for them divine love was not an emotion. Augustine defined the love of God as a function of His reason and will alone — God *feels* nothing. Thus, according to the ancient theologians, love as humans know it in an emotive sense has nothing to do with God, the statements of the scriptures notwithstanding. Neither can God have genuine *compassion* or *empathy* for human suffering, except as those terms are redefined to eliminate the element of feeling.[39] In this way the language of scripture — the bare words themselves — are retained, but their meaning is completely subverted by philosophical concerns.

Of course the greatest passion of all was the suffering of Christ in Gethsemane and on the cross. Thus the central fact of the Christian gospel was also the biggest obstacle to embracing the absolutely nonbiblical Greek ideal of an impassible God — a God who cannot suffer. This obstacle was finally overcome in 451 A.D. at the Council of Chalcedon, when the theologians declared that unlike all other entities, which have a single essence or nature, Jesus Christ must have had *two* natures, one human and one divine.[40] It was the human nature that suffered on the cross — the divine nature, the pre-existent Son of God, didn't feel a thing. The human Jesus may have suffered and died for sinners, but the divine Son of God never did!

Did the divine, pre-existent Word, God the Son, actually become human in his nature and then suffer and die for humanity? The Latter-day Saint answer is an emphatic *yes;* but the orthodox Council of Chalcedon said no, the Bible is not to be taken literally on these points.[41] According to the *Tome* of Pope Leo the Great, which was approved at the council, to pay the debt that we had incurred, an inviolable nature was united to a nature that can suffer. . . . Each nature preserves its own characteristics without diminution, so that the form of a servant does not detract from the form of God. . . . Each nature performs its proper functions in communion with the other; the Word performs what pertains to the Word, the flesh what pertains to the flesh.[42]

Thus Chalcedon provided a formula by which the theologians could maintain contradictory propositions—that God suffered, because of the corporate identity of the two natures in Christ, and that God did not suffer, because of the strict distinction between the two natures. The formula allowed orthodoxy to affirm with the New Testament that Christ suffered while agreeing with Plato that God is impassible. Most modern Christians are unaware of the doctrine at all and naively talk about a God who suffers, but those who are conversant with the fine points of orthodoxy know that according to the fourth- and fifth-century church fathers, the divine nature within Christ could not and did not suffer for us or anyone else. Henry Chadwick expresses it in this way: "The enthusiasm of devotion may say that 'God suffered and died'; but the theologian knows that God is impassible and immortal, and therefore that this transfer of human frailty to God . . . does not strictly mean what it says."[43]

The theological proposition of the two natures in Christ, an invention of the post-apostolic Church, was so incomprehensible and so controversial that it took two hundred years to finally go down, and even then the Egyptian, Abyssinian, Syrian, and Armenian churches never would swallow it. They believed that this doctrine was a cleverly disguised rejection of the central claim of the New Testament—that God suffered and died for man. Yet orthodoxy was willing to accept the doctrine of the two natures simply because Greek philosophy couldn't abide the idea of a God that suffers, either emotionally or physically, and the church at that time had more trust in the logic of its philosophers than in the literal language of its scriptures.[44]

The perception of God intuitively shared by most Christians today remains anthropomorphic as regards both his form and his ability to feel. In fact the actual perception of most Christians is closer to the LDS doctrine of God—that of an *actual* Father who *really* lives in heaven and *really* loves us—than it is to the philosophical theology taught by the councils. If the biblical anthropomorphisms and emotions attributed to God are merely allegorical and must be discarded in order to achieve a correct understanding of God's nature, shouldn't the Bible itself give some indication of that fact?

That most Christians "naively" perceive God in anthropomorphic terms doesn't necessarily argue that the anthropomorphic view of God is correct, but it does argue that if perceiving the Christian God in anthropomorphic terms renders one a non-Christian, then a majority of the people who have considered themselves Christians, like the monks of the Egyptian desert, must probably be excluded from Christianity along with the Latter-day Saints. Certainly most Christian children, even in orthodox denominations, think of God anthropomorphically until they are old enough to be taught otherwise. One could hardly argue that such children are non-Christian and unsaved until they make the conceptual adjustment to a nonanthropomorphic Deity.

A Final Question

Is it possible to have faith in everything the New Testament says about Jesus Christ and still not be a Christian? Just how adequate, how competent, is the unadorned biblical proclamation? Will the atonement of Christ be effective for someone who believes every single word of the New Testament, but believes God the Father *could* have a tangible body like his Son? Even though the New Testament is silent on the issue, will such an opinion cancel the efficacy of Christ's atonement in that person's life? Are we to believe that those who worship a Father, Son, and Holy Ghost perceived as *homoousios* (Greek for "of the same substance") will enjoy eternal bliss, while those who worship a Father, Son, and Holy Ghost perceived as *homoiousios* (Greek for "of like substance") will, as heretics, be denied the blessings of salvation, even though neither word can be found in the teachings of Jesus or his Apostles, or be found anywhere in scripture?

It is true that there were ancient heretics — Gnostics, Marcionites, and others — who rejected the New Testament or parts of it, but I'm not talking about them. I'm talking about Christians — the first-century Church, the Apostolic Fathers, and the Greek Apologists — who believed all the New Testament, every word of it, but did not share the interpretation given to it centuries later by theologians steeped in Greek philosophy. Just how adequate for salvation is unadorned New Testament Christianity,

anyway? Those critics who deny Christianity to the Latter-day
Saints for not accepting the doctrines of the councils imply that
the teachings of Jesus and the Apostles were incomplete and inadequate for salvation until supplemented and defined by the
church fathers — the "new, improved" Christianity of the fourth
and fifth centuries. Latter-day Saints see this rejection of the
primitive biblical Christianity in favor of the expanded philosophical Christianity of later times as "making the word of God
[the New Testament] of none effect through your [philosophical]
tradition" (see Mark 7:13).

Summary

The Latter-day Saints accept unequivocally all the biblical
teachings on the nature of God, but they reject the extrabiblical
elaborations of the councils and creeds. A doctrinal exclusion applied to the Latter-day Saints for rejecting the Nicene doctrine of
the Trinity is invalid because that doctrine was not taught in the
Bible or in the early Christian church. It is not found in the teachings of the Apostolic Fathers or those of the Greek Apologists.
Even today Eastern and Western orthodoxies still disagree
strongly over both the precise nature of God and the exact word-
ings of the major creed of Christianity (the *filioque* dispute). If in
order to be a true Christian one must conceive of the Christian
God in precisely the terms of Nicene orthodoxy, then all Christians who lived before the fifth century, and all those on at least
one side of the *filioque* dispute since the eighth century, must be
excluded as Christians as well as the Latter-day Saints. Moreover,
it is contradictory for Protestants to insist on the doctrine of *sola
scriptura* — that the Bible alone is sufficient for salvation — in one
context, and then to turn around and add nonscriptural requirements for salvation, like acceptance of councils and creeds, in
other contexts.

Latter-day Saints agree that God the Father is spirit in the
highest sense of the word, but they deny that this limits him to
incorporeality. God is *a* spirit in the person of the Holy Ghost, but
in the person of the Son, God has a tangible body. On the
grounds of modern revelation Latter-day Saints believe that God
the Father also has a tangible body, but they grant that this cannot be proved or disproved from the Bible. Still, given their philosophical assumptions it is the orthodox who must, without biblical warrant, dismiss the biblical anthropomorphisms applied to

God as merely figurative, while the Latter-day Saints accept them at face value. The anthropomorphic view of God is compatible with biblical imagery, but conflicts with the Greek philosophical definition of God. If conceiving of God in anthropomorphic terms, as the Latter-day Saints do, excludes one from being a Christian, then most Christians, both ancient and modern, must also be excluded, for most are guilty in some degree of conceiving of God in anthropomorphic biblical terms rather than in the abstract terms of philosophical theology. Moreover, since the Bible itself describes God in anthropomorphic language, even if such descriptions are understood merely as helpful symbolism or allegory, it cannot be seriously argued that perceiving God in anthropomorphic terms is an un-Christian practice.

8

The Doctrinal Exclusion: Lesser Arguments

Occasionally the claim has been made that the practice of polygamy is so abhorrent to all true Christians that anyone who would espouse it or even tolerate it cannot be truly Christian. It follows, the argument runs, that since many Latter-day Saints practiced plural marriage during the latter half of the nineteenth century, this practice reveals their religion to be non-Christian. The argument runs into several difficulties, however, but before we look at them we must say a few things about the LDS doctrine of plural marriage.

LDS Plural Marriage

First of all, during the period when plural marriage was practiced by the Latter-day Saints it was the exception rather than the rule. There were more monogamous marriages among the Mormons than there were polygamous marriages, and without special dispensation a Latter-day Saint could not take a plural wife.

Second, the Latter-day Saints do *not* maintain that the practice of plural marriage is a requirement for entrance into the kingdom of God, nor do they argue that plural marriage is taught in the New Testament.[1] While Latter-day Saints do believe that whenever God commands the Saints must obey, they do not insist that plural marriage is an essential element of the gospel of

Jesus Christ or that plural marriage is intrinsically preferable to monogamy.[2] The atonement of Christ will save or exalt a monogamist as readily as a polygamist, and vice versa.

Third, because plural marriage is neither a universal nor an essential principle of the gospel, the Lord may command, tolerate, or forbid the practice among his people as their circumstances warrant. For example, in the Book of Mormon itself (Jacob 2:27–28) the Lord *forbade* plural marriage to the Nephites, though apparently the practice had been allowed to Israelites generally under the law of Moses. Conversely, in the nineteenth century the Lord *commanded* that plural marriage be practiced among the Latter-day Saints; thus LDS plural marriage was not the result of some scriptural discovery or a doctrinal preference for polygamy, but was due to the direct command of God in revelation to the Prophet Joseph Smith. For Latter-day Saints plural marriage of itself has nothing to commend it, but the command of the Lord makes the practice right or wrong. What the Lord requires is right; what he forbids is wrong.[3] The question before us here, however, is not whether plural marriage is right or wrong, but whether merely believing that it *can* be right under special circumstances necessarily renders one non-Christian.

The Abhorrence of Plural Marriage

To abhor plural marriage is not the same thing as merely not to practice it. Even in cultures where polygamy is allowed, the majority of people generally choose not to practice it, yet they are not horrified by those who do. In Western culture plural marriage is generally abhorred, but the roots of this abhorrence can hardly be described as biblical, for the Old Testament explicitly sanctions polygamy,[4] and the New Testament does not forbid it. The practice could not have been abhorrent to Jesus and the first-century Jewish Christians, for their culture was not Western, and plural marriage was sanctioned in the law of Moses,[5] the holiness of which was endorsed by both Jesus and Paul.[6] Indeed, it is possible that some Jewish Christians of the first century continued to practice plural marriage just as they continued Sabbath observance, circumcision, and other practices related to their cultural and religious background. The cultural milieu of Judaism and early Christianity simply cannot be the source of the Western horror of plural marriage, for plural marriages were common in the environment of the earliest Christian church.

I do not deny that polygamy is now abhorred in Western culture generally and in modern Christianity particularly. What I deny is that the source of that abhorrence is biblical. It is derived not from the biblical heritage but the classical—the abhorrence of polygamy comes from Greece and Rome.[7] As orthodox a figure as Saint Augustine knew that the prohibition of plural marriage in the church of his day was only a matter of Roman custom: "Again, Jacob the son of Isaac is charged with having committed a great crime because he had four wives. But here there is no ground for a criminal accusation: for a plurality of wives was no crime when it was the custom; and it is a crime now, because it is no longer the custom. . . . The only reason of its being a crime now to do this, is because custom and the laws forbid it."[8] Though pagan culture could freely tolerate multiple sexual partners, it could tolerate only one wife. In that respect Greco-Roman culture was very similar to contemporary Western culture.

Clearly, then, the antagonism to plural marriage was not biblical in origin, for the bosom of Abraham, where most Christians long to repose, is a polygamous bosom, and the house of Israel, into which most Christians seek admission, is a polygamous house.

Polygamy and Divorce

Now, it has been argued that the Old Testament approval of plural marriage should be understood as being analogous to its toleration of divorce, that both practices were permitted to the Jewish people under the Mosaic law only because of their moral weakness, and that both practices were later prohibited to Christians. Yet while the New Testament makes such a statement about divorce (Matthew 19:3–9), nowhere does it make such a statement about plural marriage; there is no biblical warrant for equating the two cases.

But even if there were such a warrant, there are at least two reasons why equating divorce and plural marriage would not help the excluders' argument—in fact such an analogy would make *my* case. First, the New Testament indicates that while divorce was prohibited generally, it was allowed in special circumstances (Matthew 19:9; 1 Corinthians 7:15, the so-called Pauline privilege). This is all the Latter-day Saints would claim for the practice of plural marriage—that it is prohibited generally but allowed under special circumstances. Second, if the practice of plural marriage is analogous to the practice of divorce, and today there are literally millions of divorced Christians, why can there be no polygamous Christians? In truth, despite the fact that it is specifically prohibited in the New Testament, for most Christian denominations divorce is no bar to membership, though it may be discouraged or disapproved of. I am personally acquainted with several divorced Protestant ministers. But if divorce and plural marriage are to be understood as analogous cases, then the sanctions against plural marriage, which is *not* specifically prohibited in scripture, cannot reasonably be greater than those against divorce, which *is* prohibited. Further, divorced persons are still generally accepted as Christians by their contemporary churches, and rightly so. But if divorce and plural marriage really are analogous, then those who merely believe in the possibility of plural marriage (without practicing it, I might add) should be accepted as Christians as readily as those who actually practice divorce.

Christian Precedents

Once again, I am not arguing that plural marriage is correct. I am only arguing that believing it *could* be right under special circumstances does not render one a non-Christian. Robert Holst, a Protestant missionary to New Guinea, notes that in that country "Baptist and Methodist missions baptize those who entered a polygamous marriage before coming into contact with the Gospel or, more specifically, before making a decision to accept Christ. They do not consider polygamy a sin but feel that it is not the ideal of God.''[9] In other words, the missionaries believed that polygamy is not a bar in all circumstances to being a Christian. Shall we write off both the converts and their missionaries for believing that in some circumstances plural marriage can be tolerated in a Christian church?

Protestants in other areas have similarly argued for the possibility of Christian polygamists: "Let it be publicly declared that a polygamous African church may still be classified as a Christian church, even while monogamy remains the Christian norm, and that no such church will be excluded from Christian councils and full Christian fellowship solely because of its polygamy.''[10]

Perhaps the best illustration of the possibility of Christian plural marriage is provided by the great Reformer himself, Martin Luther. There is no doubt that Luther was *generally* opposed to the practice of plural marriage: "Consequently it is my opinion that a Christian is not free to marry several wives *unless God commands him* to go beyond the liberty which is conditioned by love.''[11] But it is just as consistently clear that in Luther's theology opposition to plural marriage was never absolute. Even where he wrote in favor of monogamy Luther generally added that polygamy could be allowed to a Christian under special circumstances; for example, if a wife should contract leprosy, or if she should be unwilling to engage in marital relations, or if there was ''some other compelling reason''[12] — or, as stated above, if ''God commands him.'' By contrast, in the LDS view only the latter contingency would justify an exception to monogamy. Without a specific commandment from God, plural marriage is as unacceptable for the Latter-day Saints as it is for other Christians, an offense for which excommunication is the certain result.

But there were other circumstances in which Luther thought plural marriage allowable. In September 1531 Luther wrote a letter to Robert Barnes — the envoy of the English king Henry VIII — who had been seeking Luther's support for Henry's divorce from Catherine of Aragon. In it Luther argued that since divorce was forbidden by God and would be unjust to Catherine, Henry should simply marry a second wife.[13]

Eight years later one of Luther's supporters, Philip, the Landgrave of Hesse, desired to marry Margarete von der Saale without divorcing his first wife (since divorce was prohibited in scripture). Neither Philip nor the prospective bride and her mother would go ahead with the plural marriage, however, without the written sanction of the Lutheran theologians. On 10 December 1539 Luther, Bucer, Melanchthon, and others signed a document stipulating that the proposed plural marriage was acceptable, ''since the Gospel neither revokes nor forbids what was permitted in the Law of Moses with respect to marriage.'' After being strongly advised to keep the whole thing secret for understandable political and cultural reasons, Philip was further assured (in writing) that he had ''the approval of us all'' in his proposed plural marriage.[14] Consequently the marriage was performed on 4 March 1540 by Dennis Melander, the Lutheran court chaplain, with Bucer and Melanchthon present.[15]

I do not mean here to represent Luther as a champion of plural marriage. For him monogamy was clearly the rule — but polygamy was an allowable exception to Luther's rule, a viable option in special circumstances. It should be carefully noted that Luther much preferred polygamy to divorce, yet many modern Christians, while abhorring polygamy, practice divorce as though it were almost a Christian sacrament.

My point is this: If Luther could seriously endorse plural marriage, in writing, on at least two occasions almost a decade apart; if he could certify in writing that the plural marriage of Philip of Hesse was acceptable in the context of the Christian gospel; and if he could then sanction the actual marriage itself; then I feel it safe to say that Martin Luther sanctioned plural marriage under special circumstances. And if he is still to be counted a Christian, as he most assuredly is, then it is not true that endorsing plural marriage under any circumstances renders one a non-Christian. If Luther, Bucer, and Melanchthon could advise and sanction plural marriages and remain Christians, then so could Joseph Smith and Brigham Young.

The Esoteric Teaching (the Temple)

Another issue used by those who employ the doctrinal exclusion involves the esoteric teaching of LDS temple worship. Those who have received this teaching are under a covenant obligation not to discuss the details of the LDS temple and its ordinances. This makes attacking them on the subject similar to debating a monk under a vow of silence — it is usually an easy victory, but never a heroic one. It is not necessary to discuss or defend the LDS temple in detail here, however, for the charge of the non-LDS critics is not that the LDS version of the esoteric teaching in Christianity is incorrect (that would be an interdenominational squabble), but rather that there *never was* an esoteric teaching in Christianity at all, and that anyone who believes in an esoteric teaching is therefore not a Christian.

An esoteric teaching is any teaching that is held back from general, public circulation, a teaching not available to everyone but reserved for the initiated. In the LDS context this also involves vicarious ordinances for the dead. The question before us is not whether the specific LDS esoteric teaching is the right one, but whether Christianity ever had any kind of an esoteric teaching at all. For if it did, then it is a *Christian* phenomenon — whether the modern denominations have it or not, and whether the LDS understanding of it is correct or not.

The Esoteric Teaching in the New Testament

Let's begin with the Apostle Paul, who wrote in his First Epistle to the Corinthians: ''Howbeit we speak wisdom among them that are perfect: yet not the wisdom of this world, nor of the princes of this world, that come to nought: but we speak the wisdom of God in a mystery, even the hidden wisdom, which God ordained before the world unto our glory" (1 Corinthians 2:6-7). The Greek word translated "perfect" in verse 6 is *teleios*, and besides "perfect" it also means "mature" and "initiated."[16] So for Paul there is a hidden wisdom communicated not to the masses but only to those who are mature. By definition this is an esoteric teaching, an esoteric teaching communicated, Paul says, "in a mystery." The Greek word translated "mystery" is *musterion*, and it means "a mystery," "a secret," "a secret rite," or "a secret teaching."[17] Thus here we have in the New Testament a hidden wisdom communicated by means of a secret rite (*musterion*) only to those who are mature or initiated. Even if there were no other evidence, this passage alone would prove the existence of an esoteric teaching in earliest Christianity. As one non-LDS scholar has remarked: "Paul reveals here almost certainly that he knew an esoteric Christian apocalyptic-wisdom teaching which he carefully guarded from immature Christians."[18]

Some commentators on these verses have tried to argue that the public Christian proclamation itself was the hidden wisdom, but that argument is untenable for two reasons. First, the Christian proclamation was not hidden or reserved only for the mature; it was preached "upon the housetops." Second, while the Corinthian Saints had already heard the Christian proclamation and been converted and baptized, Paul felt that they still were not yet mature enough for the "meat" of the gospel. Therefore the two levels of teachings, the public and the hidden, cannot be equivalent. "And I, brethren, could not speak unto you as unto spiritual, but as unto carnal, even as unto babes in Christ. I have fed you with milk, and not with meat: for hitherto ye were not able to bear it, neither yet now are ye able." (1 Corinthians 3:1-2.) Since the Corinthians were already Christians, the meat which Paul continued to withhold from them cannot have been the public Christian proclamation.[19] Whatever it was, the fact that it was withheld from them because they were not yet ready for it makes it by definition an esoteric teaching.

In the Second Epistle to the Corinthians, Paul refers to secret teachings he received by revelation when he was caught up to the third heaven—"how that he was caught up into paradise, and heard unspeakable words, which it is not lawful for a man to utter" (2 Corinthians 12:4). What Paul learned on this occasion was certainly esoteric, and I think we may assume that not all Christians have received it. Moreover, Paul felt obliged to keep these things secret, no doubt "because they are too sacred"[20] to be written or told.

In 1 Corinthians, Paul also refers to an early Christian practice of vicarious baptism for the dead, which is one of the rites of the LDS temples. While arguing that without the resurrection of Christ and of all mankind, faith and repentance and even his own preaching are all in vain, he asks: "Else what shall they do which are baptized for the dead, if the dead rise not at all? why are they then baptized for the dead?" (1 Corinthians 15:29.) Scholars and theologians have proposed many different theories to try and explain this verse. Yet honest scholars, both Catholic and Protestant (even those hostile to the LDS doctrine), are forced to admit that the passage describes vicarious baptism for the dead, and that proposed alternatives are really just attempts to *avoid* the clear meaning of the text because of its theological implications.

Regarding 1 Corinthians 15:29, a conservative Protestant work explains: "The normal reading of the text is that some Corinthians are being baptized, apparently vicariously, in behalf of some people who have already died. It would be fair to add that this reading is such a plain understanding of the Greek text that no one would ever have imagined the various alternatives were it not for the difficulties involved."[21] The finest Roman Catholic biblical commentary is of the same opinion: "Again, the Apostle alludes to a practice of the Corinthian community as evidence for a Christian faith in the resurrection of the dead. It seems that in Corinth some Christians would undergo baptism in the name of their deceased non-Christian relatives and friends, hoping that this vicarious baptism might assure them a share in the redemption of Christ."[22]

Both Catholic and Protestant scholars agree that the Corinthian Saints practiced baptism for the dead. Now, the argument is sometimes made that Paul must have merely tolerated an aberrant practice at Corinth, that he looked the other way because these vicarious baptisms reflected a kind of faith in Christ. There are serious problems with this view, even from a non-LDS perspective. But even if the argument were valid, Latter-day Saints would be entitled to ask their critics, If the Apostle Paul found vicarious rites for the dead tolerable among the Corinthian Saints, why must the same practice be judged intolerable among the Latter-day Saints? If the Bible shows that the Apostle Paul was in fellowship with those who, rightly or wrongly, practiced baptism for the dead, how can modern Christians reject the precedent?

The Esoteric Teaching in Early Christianity

In the centuries following Paul many other orthodox writers refer to the esoteric teaching. In fact one scholarly source states that Saint Clement of Alexandria, the head of the catechetical school at Alexandria and the most influential theologian of his generation, "based his exegesis on the existence of a Christian gnosis, i.e., the secret knowledge of the profoundest truths of the Christian faith to which the elite were initiated."[23]

Clement's writings were never anathematized by any council, and he is still revered as an orthodox saint by several modern denominations.[24] Yet Eusebius of Caesarea quotes him as saying: "James the Righteous, John, and Peter were entrusted by the Lord after his resurrection with the higher knowledge. They imparted it to the other apostles, and the other apostles to the Seventy."[25] This "higher knowledge" cannot be the public gospel message, for the teaching described here was not given directly by Christ to the disciples as was the public teaching, but was a separate revelation communicated privately only through Peter, James, and John. Clement often refers to the public Christian message as "the common faith," "the foundation," or "the milk."[26] The esoteric teaching he refers to as "the higher knowledge," "the secret things," or "the gnosis." For example, Clement explains:

> The Lord did not hinder from doing good while keeping the Sabbath; but allowed us to communicate of those divine mysteries, and of that holy light, to those who are able to receive them. He did not certainly disclose to the many what did not belong to the many; but to the few to whom He knew that they belonged, who were capable of receiving and being moulded according to them. But secret things are entrusted to speech, not to writing, as is the case with God.[27]

For centuries orthodox interpreters of Clement's writings have insisted that there wasn't really any esoteric teaching in his theology, but that the so-called "secret teaching" was merely the public message itself, which was understood by different believers according to their different capacities. The mature understood the public gospel well, and the immature understood it less well. But since 1973, that dodge has been no longer possible, for in that year a previously unknown letter of Clement was published[28] that makes matters quite clear. Following is an excerpt from that letter as translated by Morton Smith (notes for this quotation are mine; square brackets are in the original):

> Mark, then, during Peter's stay in Rome, he wrote [an account of] the Lord's doings,* not, however, declaring all [of them], nor yet hinting at the secret [ones], but selecting those he thought most useful for increasing the faith of those who were being instructed. But when Peter died as a martyr, Mark came over to Alexandria, bringing both his own notes and those of Peter, from which he transferred to his former book the things suitable to whatever makes for progress toward knowledge [*gnosis*]. [Thus] he composed a more spiritual Gospel† for the use of those who were being perfected.[29] Nevertheless, he yet did not divulge the things not to be uttered, nor did he write down the hierophantic[30] teaching of the Lord, but to the stories already written he added yet others and, moreover, brought in certain sayings of which he knew the interpretation would, as a mystagogue,[31] lead the hearers into the innermost sanctuary of that truth hidden by seven [veils][32]. . . . and, dying, he left his composition to the church in Alexandria, where it even yet is most carefully guarded, being read only to those who are being initiated into the great mysteries.[33]

In view of this letter, which a large majority of scholars now accept as genuine,[34] it is no longer possible to argue that Clement did not believe in an esoteric teaching in precisely the LDS sense. In this Secret Gospel of Mark, as it is now called, the esoteric teaching was not the public gospel, but was an *addition* to what was contained in the canonical Gospel of Mark. Even so, Clement informs his reader, there were secrets even beyond those — secrets he calls "the hierophantic teaching of the Lord" — which were too sacred to be written down even in the Secret Gospel.

In the same letter Clement goes on to explain that the Carpocratians and other Gnostics erred, not by their inventing an esoteric teaching out of thin air but by their distorting the *genuine* esoteric teachings of Christianity.

---

*I.e., the canonical Gospel of Mark.
†I.e., a Secret Gospel of Mark.

Now, Clement's letter does not prove that there was a Secret Gospel written by Mark, although it certainly establishes the possibility. The letter *does* prove, however, that Saint Clement, the foremost orthodox theologian of his generation and head of the catechetical school at Alexandria, *believed* there was an entirely orthodox Secret Gospel, and since he claims to have read it, he himself must have been "initiated into the great mysteries." Moreover, he cannot have been the only orthodox Christian in Alexandria to have so believed or to have been so initiated. Alexandrian orthodoxy of the second century included, at least among the "mature" Christians of Alexandria, a belief in an esoteric Christian teaching. This is now simply a matter of record.

In the fourth century the emperor Constantine built churches on the three holiest sites in Christendom: the locations of the Nativity, the Resurrection, and the Ascension. Concerning the third of these churches, which was called anciently the Eleona, Eusebius, the "Father of Church History" and an orthodox theologian, writes: "The mother of the emperor raised a stately structure on the Mount of Olives also, in memory of his ascent to heaven who is the Saviour of mankind, erecting a sacred church and temple on the very summit of the mount. And indeed authentic history informs us that in this very cave the Saviour imparted his secret revelations to his disciples."[35]

Shortly thereafter Saint Cyril of Jerusalem described a baptismal ceremony that can only be described as an esoteric rite of initiation.[36] Both the details of the ritual itself and Cyril's mystical interpretation of it were to be kept strictly secret:

When the instruction is over, if any catechumen tries to get out of you what your teachers told you, tell nothing, for he is outside the mystery that we have delivered to you, with its hope of the age to come. Guard the mystery for his sake from whom you look for reward. Never let anyone persuade you, saying "What harm is it that I should know as well?" . . . Already you stand on the frontier of mystery. I adjure you to smuggle no word out.[37]

As Cyril describes the action of the mystery, first "you stretched forth your hand and, as though Satan were present, you renounced him."[38] Until the ordinances were complete, "the men were to stay with the men and the women with the women."[39] The initiates were then anointed with consecrated oil in stages from their forehead, ears, nose, and so on, down to their feet.[40] Cyril describes this as the anointing referred to in the New Testament at 1 John 2:20, 27.[41] After being anointed the initiates were washed in baptism three times, were anointed again, and then were dressed in white robes that Cyril calls "the garment of salvation."[42] The initiates received the name of Christian—in fact Cyril calls them "Christs"[43]—and they passed from an "outer" to an "inner" chamber, which Cyril calls in unmistakable temple symbolism the "Holy of Holies."[44]

Cyril of Jerusalem was not alone in teaching this esoteric doctrine. Saint Ambrose of Milan (Saint Augustine's teacher), Saint John Chrysostom in Constantinople, and Theodore of Mopsuestia are just a few of the Fathers who taught essentially the same things in widely separated geographical areas of the Christian church.[45]

Saint Basil (the Great) also wrote of secret teachings that were separate and distinct from the written gospel and that had been passed down from the Apostles:

> Of the beliefs and practices whether generally accepted or publicly enjoined which are preserved in the Church some we possess derived from written teaching; others we have received delivered to us "in a mystery" by the tradition of the apostles; and both of these in relation to true religion have the same force. . . . For we are not, as is well known, content with what the apostle or the Gospel has recorded, but both in preface and conclusion we add other words as being of great importance to the validity of the ministry, and these we derive from unwritten teaching. . . . Nay, by what written word is the anointing of oil itself taught? . . . Does not this come from that unpublished and secret teaching which our fathers guarded in a silence out of the reach of curious meddling and inquisitive investigation? Well had they learnt the lesson that the awful dignity of the mysteries is best preserved by silence. What the uninitiated are not even allowed to look at was hardly likely to be publicly paraded about in written documents.[46]

Now, some modern Christians may dismiss all of this as hocus-pocus, but these things were performed in great seriousness over a period of centuries by orthodox Christians who understood them as sacred teachings of the gospel, teachings considered to be over and above what was contained in the written New Testament. Basil and Cyril were Christian *saints*; Basil wrote the discipline for monastic life that is still the rule in Orthodoxy; and Cyril attended the Council of Constantinople in A.D. 381 and helped to formulate its version of the Nicene Creed. Moreover, Cyril's lectures on the secret teachings were delivered to the initiates in the Church of the Holy Sepulchre in Jerusalem—the holiest shrine of orthodoxy.[47] These men and their esoteric teachings cannot be dismissed as unorthodox.

My point is this: If objective scholars can conclude that the New Testament supports an esoteric teaching in Paul; if the New Testament explicitly states that Corinthian Christians practiced vicarious baptism for the dead; if Saint Clement of Alexandria believed that an esoteric teaching of the Lord was part of Christianity, and Clement himself had been initiated into it; if Saint Basil can emphatically state that the most sacred Christian teachings were never written down but were found in secret rites and teachings handed down from the Apostles; if Saint Cyril of Jerusalem could perform secret rituals and in the Church of the Holy Sepulchre instruct his initiates on the esoteric meanings of those rituals; then there is no case for excluding the Latter-day Saints from Christendom simply because they believe in an esoteric teaching.

Though modern Christians are often embarrassed by the fact, it is a matter of historical record that esoteric teachings have been part of orthodox Christian practice in other times and places. Modern Christians might reject the views of Clement, Basil, Cyril, Ambrose, Chrysostom, and the other Fathers, and even accuse them of being influenced by the pagan mysteries—but normally they don't accuse them of *being* pagans. And if an esoteric teaching is going to be tolerated in the orthodox church of the third, fourth, and fifth centuries, there is no reason it can't be tolerated in the modern Latter-day Saints.

The Premortal Existence of Souls

Another doctrine of the Latter-day Saints that sometimes comes under attack and is used to exclude them from Christian circles is the premortal existence of souls.

One would think that the orthodox doctrine of the soul would have been established firmly in the earliest periods of the Christian era or in the New Testament itself, but this is hardly the case. One informative reference source explains: ''No precise teaching about the soul received general acceptance in the Christian Church until the Middle Ages. The Scriptures are explicit only on the facts of the distinction between soul and body, the creation of the soul of the first man by the Divine breath, and its immortality.''[48] Christians still disagree on the exact nature of the soul, and several different theories of how souls are created coexist among the modern Christian churches.

On the basis of modern revelation the Latter-day Saints believe that all souls (Latter-day Saints often call them ''spirits'') were organized in a premortal existence and that they lived for a time in the presence of God *before* they came to earth to inhabit their individual bodies. This view is sometimes misunderstood by non-LDS people as a belief in reincarnation or in the transmigration of souls, but the Latter-day Saints are hostile to both of those doctrines; for in LDS belief once a soul has received a mortal body, it cannot enter another mortal body. The only difference here between the beliefs of Latter-day Saints and those of other Christians concerns whether souls are created individually at the moment of conception or of birth, or whether they were created before that moment. Other Christians may disagree with the Latter-day Saints, but since Christians interpret differently the few Bible references on this issue, and since the traditional views — themselves surmises — weren't commonly accepted until the Middle Ages, the claim that one's whole standing as a Christian hangs on believing one or the other is exceedingly weak.

How We Are Saved

One sometimes hears that Latter-day Saints aren't Christians because all true Christians believe in salvation by grace, while the Mormons believe in salvation by works. If this were true, it would mean that Mormons believe each individual ''works out his own salvation.'' Under such a belief, salvation becomes an individual accomplishment — something each one does to and for himself or herself — while the atonement of Christ becomes merely a handy tool to be used by the individual in his or her own do-it-yourself salvation kit. Those who view salvation in this way — and apparently there are some misinformed Latter-day Saints who do — in effect say, ''And surely *I* will do it; wherefore give *me* thine honor.''[49] Salvation ceases to be the greatest of all the *gifts* of God (D&C 6:13) and becomes something an individual earns for himself by simply following the proper steps or numbers. Under this view Christ is dethroned as a personal Savior, as the one who actually accomplishes the work of individual salvation, and salvation is no longer a Christ-centered but rather a self-centered activity.

My first observation regarding this idea of salvation by works is that it has nothing to do with LDS doctrine. In fact it could have been treated in chapter 2 of this book, for the charge that this is what Latter-day Saints believe badly misrepresents the LDS position. Now, even among non-LDS Christians the doctrine of divine grace can be hotly argued, so I will not attempt to define that doctrine to the satisfaction of all non-LDS critics. Nevertheless, the following basic principles taken from the Book of Mormon do, I believe, provide a fair representation of the LDS view.[50]

First, it is impossible to *earn* or *deserve* any of the blessings of God in any sense that leaves the individual unindebted to God's grace. In the Book of Mormon, King Benjamin expresses it in this way:

> I say unto you that if ye should serve him who has created you from the beginning, and is preserving you from day to day, by lending you breath, that ye may live and move and do according to your own will, and even supporting you from one moment to another—I say, if ye should serve him with all your whole souls yet ye would be unprofitable servants. . . .
>
> . . . And ye are still indebted unto him, and are, and will be, forever and ever; therefore, of what have ye to boast? (Mosiah 2:21, 24.)

Even in those contexts, such as the law of tithing, where there is a *quid pro quo*—a covenant agreement that if I will do A, God will grant B—the very fact that such a covenant has been offered to me and that I am able to receive such overwhelming blessings in return for such paltry efforts is in itself a prior act of grace—an expression of the pure love of God, a gift. Salvation itself is the result of such a covenant of grace—"the new testament [covenant] in my blood" (Luke 22:20). The very existence of this covenant is a gift, a grace offered by a volunteer Savior. Yet like all covenants, there are terms binding upon both parties. Our best efforts to live the laws of God are required, but not because they

earn the promised rewards—our efforts are infinitely dispropor-
tionate to the actual costs. Rather, our best efforts are a token of
our good faith and of our acceptance of the offered covenant.
Thus we participate in our own salvation as we attempt to keep
the commandments of God, but we can never earn it ourselves or
bring it to pass on our own merits, no matter how well we may
think we are doing.

Second, redemption can never come as the result of an indi-
vidual's own efforts, but only through the atonement of Jesus
Christ. The Book of Mormon prophet Lehi explains this to his son
Jacob:

> Wherefore, I know that thou art redeemed, because of the
> righteousness of thy Redeemer. . . .
>
> And men are instructed sufficiently that they know
> good from evil. And the law is given unto men. And by
> the law no flesh is justified; or, by the law men are cut
> off. . . .
>
> Wherefore, redemption cometh in and through the
> Holy Messiah; for he is full of grace and truth.
>
> Behold, he offereth himself a sacrifice for sin, to
> answer the ends of the law, unto all those who have a
> broken heart and a contrite spirit; and unto none else can
> the ends of the law be answered.
>
> Wherefore, how great the importance to make these
> things known unto the inhabitants of the earth, that they
> may know that there is no flesh that can dwell in the pres-
> ence of God, save it be through the merits, and mercy, and
> grace of the Holy Messiah. (2 Nephi 2:3, 5–8.)

There is no doctrine, ritual, principle, ordinance, law, perform-
ance, church, belief, program, angel, or prophet that can save us
in the absence of the personal intervention in our lives of the
Lord and Savior Jesus Christ. This is the teaching of the Book of
Mormon as well as of the Bible.

Third, the individual must be born again through the atonement of Jesus Christ and become Christ's spiritual offspring. His
people having made a covenant to obey God, King Benjamin tells
them:

> And now, because of the covenant which ye have
> made ye shall be called the children of Christ, his sons,

and his daughters; for behold, this day he hath spiritually begotten you; for ye say that your hearts are changed through faith on his name; therefore, ye are born of him and have become his sons and his daughters.

And under this head ye are made free, and there is no other head whereby ye can be made free. There is no other name given whereby salvation cometh; therefore, I would that ye should take upon you the name of Christ, all you that have entered into the covenant with God that ye should be obedient unto the end of your lives. (Mosiah 5:7–8.)

Even membership in the Church of Christ is insufficient for salvation without that personal experience of the Savior and of his atonement, which begets us spiritually. Alma, another Book of Mormon prophet, makes this clear through a set of poignant questions, including the following: "And now behold, I ask of you, my brethren of the church, have ye spiritually been born of God? Have ye received his image in your countenances? Have ye experienced this mighty change in your hearts? Do ye exercise faith in the redemption of him who created you?" (Alma 5:14–15.)

Fourth, we are saved by grace and condemned without it, no matter what else we might have or do. Grace is a *sine qua non*, an essential condition, for salvation. Nephi, son of Lehi, testifies, "For we labor diligently to write, to persuade our children, and also our brethren, to believe in Christ, and to be reconciled to God; for we know that it is by grace that we are saved, after all we can do" (2 Nephi 25:23).[51] Moreover, if a person is willing to come to Christ and endure to the end, the Savior's grace is sufficient for that person's salvation, despite his or her mortal weaknesses. The Book of Mormon records these gracious words of the Lord: "And if men come unto me I will show unto them their weakness. I give unto men weakness that they may be humble; and my grace is sufficient for all men that humble themselves before me; for if they humble themselves before me, and have faith in me, then will I make weak things become strong unto them." (Ether 12:27.) In other words, our comparative righteousness is secondary in importance to our humbling ourselves, admitting our weaknesses, striving to live the gospel, and having faith in our Savior. In fact the final plea of the prophet Moroni in the last chapter of the Book of Mormon is:

Yea, come unto Christ, and be perfected in him, and deny yourselves of all ungodliness; and if ye shall deny yourselves of all ungodliness, and love God with all your might, mind and strength, then is his grace sufficient for you, that by his grace ye may be perfect in Christ; and if by the grace of God ye are perfect in Christ, ye can in nowise deny the power of God.

And again, if ye by the grace of God are perfect in Christ, and deny not his power, then are ye sanctified in Christ by the grace of God, through the shedding of the blood of Christ, which is in the covenant of the Father unto the remission of your sins, that ye become holy, without spot. (Moroni 10:32–33.)

Some critics may object that the Latter-day Saints do not insist that we are saved by grace *alone,* or do not accept the idea of *irresistible* grace (predestination), but these are points upon which other Christian denominations have disagreed as well. The specific LDS view may be right or wrong from the viewpoint of a particular denomination, but the fundamental LDS belief regarding grace and works is well within the spectrum of traditional Christianity, with strong affinities to the Wesleyan position. While not every Christian will agree with the specific LDS concept of grace, the Latter-day Saints have never believed in salvation by any other means — and especially not by individual works. It is true, I suppose, that some Latter-day Saints do not adequately understand this aspect of their own religion, but the same could be said about a minority in any denomination. The LDS scriptures are clear — we are saved by grace.

Summary

Even though the practice of plural marriage is viewed with abhorrence in Western culture, the roots of that abhorrence are not biblical. Even so, the Latter-day Saints themselves are opposed to the practice except when God commands it. Since the Western taboo against plural marriage is not biblical, and since other non-LDS Christian leaders have allowed plural marriage in special circumstances without ceasing to be Christian in the common estimation, the practice of plural marriage by a minority of Latter-day Saints (who acted in the belief that God commanded it) cannot properly be used to exclude all Latter-day Saints from Christendom.

On the basis of modern revelation the Latter-day Saints believe that the ordinances of the LDS temple, an esoteric tradition, are part of the fulness of the Christian gospel. This offends some modern Christians who believe that all genuine Christian beliefs and practices must be found in the public message of the written scriptures. This view, however, is ecclesiastically very short-sighted, for from Paul in the first century to Clement of Alexandria in the second, to the church fathers in the third and fourth, it is undeniable that an esoteric tradition—not contained in the written documents of the church but supposedly handed down from the Apostles in secret rites and teachings—was not only tolerated but fully embraced by mainstream orthodoxy for over half a millennium. It is not possible to exclude Latter-day Saints from Christendom on the basis of an esoteric teaching without excluding at the same time the very Christian Fathers whose writings have defined the nature of Christian orthodoxy.

Because the Bible is silent on *how* souls are created, modern Christians have agreed to disagree among themselves on the issue, some holding one view and some holding another. The Bible is also virtually silent about *when* souls are created; thus, by analogy, it would seem fair to agree to disagree on this issue as well, with the Latter-day Saints holding one view (that souls were created *before* the physical body), and other Christians holding a different view (that souls are created *with* the physical body). It is not a question over which one's soul, or one's Christianity, may reasonably be said to be in jeopardy.

Finally, the charge that Latter-day Saints believe in salvation by works is simply not true. That human beings can save themselves by their own efforts is contrary to the teachings of the Book of Mormon, which eloquently states the doctrine of salvation by grace. On this issue LDS doctrines are well within the spectrum of views generally accepted as Christian.

9

Conclusions

Surely by now it will have dawned on the discerning reader that of all the various arguments against Latter-day Saints being considered Christians, not one—not a *single* one—claims that Latter-day Saints don't acknowledge Jesus Christ as Lord. Consider the enormous implications of this fact. The only issue that really matters is the only issue that is carefully avoided! Picture for a moment two men arguing in front of a policeman over the contents of a box. The first man insists that his wallet, stolen by the second, is inside the box. The second man insists that the box he holds is empty and presents the officer with dozens of arguments to prove it, arguments based on everything from average wind speed at the vernal equinox to the specific gravity of applesauce. But whenever he is asked to open the box, he changes the subject with additional arguments for its being empty—all the while keeping the lid securely shut.

When the charge is made that "Mormons aren't Christians," the very first impression created in the mind of the average individual is that Latter-day Saints don't believe in Jesus Christ. Most often those who make this charge *intend* that their uninformed hearers or readers will get this impression. Yet in the arguments offered to support the assertion the only issue that really matters is never even raised: Do the Latter-day Saints believe in Jesus Christ? Do they accept him as Lord? Do they believe that he is the way, the truth, and the life, and that no man cometh unto the Father but by him? These crucial questions are never asked. And why aren't they? Because these critics of the Latter-day Saints know that to open the box is to lose the argument, for no one who is even remotely familiar with the beliefs of the Latter-day Saints — not even their most hostile critics — can deny the Latter-day Saints' belief in Jesus Christ as the Son of God, as the Savior of the world, and as the only source of salvation available to human beings.[1]

As Joseph Smith said in the very first LDS article of faith, "We believe in God, the Eternal Father, and in His Son, Jesus Christ, and in the Holy Ghost." This is amplified in the fourth article of faith by the assertion that of the first principles and ordinances of the gospel, the *very* first is "faith in the Lord Jesus Christ."

In fact Latter-day Saints go to church every Sunday with but one major purpose:

> It is expedient that the church meet together often to partake of bread and wine in the remembrance of the Lord Jesus;
>
> And the elder or priest shall administer it; and after this manner shall he administer it — he shall kneel with the church and call upon the Father in solemn prayer, saying:
>
> O God, the Eternal Father, we ask thee in the name of thy Son, Jesus Christ, to bless and sanctify this bread to the souls of all those who partake of it, that they may eat in remembrance of the body of thy Son, and witness unto thee, O God, the Eternal Father, that they are willing to take upon them the name of thy Son, and always remember him and keep his commandments which he has given them; that they may always have his Spirit to be with them. Amen. (D&C 20:75–77.)

This is done in every LDS meetinghouse practically every Sunday of the year.[2] The main purpose, the central focus of LDS Sunday services is to renew our faith in and our commitment to the Lord Jesus Christ, the Son of God. This is not a pretense or a sham; it is at the heart of what we do as Latter-day Saints.

Nor do the LDS scriptures teach anything about Christ that the rest of the Christian world would find offensive. I have frequently asked non-LDS critics exactly *which* Book of Mormon teachings about Jesus Christ they disagreed with. Invariably the response has been that it isn't *what* the Book of Mormon says or teaches per se that is offensive — it is the Book of Mormon *itself* that is offensive.

The objective observer will notice that in most cases anti-Mormons hate the LDS scriptures generically, without knowing or caring what those scriptures actually teach about Christ, simply because Latter-day Saints dare to call them "scriptures." You see, it isn't really the LDS doctrine of Christ that is objectionable; rather it is the claim that Joseph Smith was a prophet of God and that the Book of Mormon is God's word. If Joseph had never claimed to be a prophet and if he had advertised the Book of Mormon as merely his own scriptural commentary, like those of Calvin and Luther, instead of claiming it to be scripture, the Book of Mormon doctrine of Christ would have been considered quite unobjectionable by contemporary standards.

In fact, to use the terminology of biblical scholars, the Latter-day Saints have a very high Christology. That is, for the Latter-day Saints Jesus is not merely a good man, a teacher, or even a prophet; he is not merely a human being; he is not the son of Joseph and Mary who later became God's Son. In common with other Bible-oriented Christians, the Latter-day Saints believe that Jesus is the pre-existent Word of the Father who became the literal, physical, genetic Son of God. As the pre-existent Word he was the agent of the Father in the creation of all things. As the glorified Son he is the agent of the Father in the salvation of all humanity. We believe he was conceived of a virgin by the power of the Holy Ghost. We believe he led a sinless life, that he was morally and ethically perfect, that he healed the sick and raised the dead, that he walked on the water and multiplied the loaves and the fishes. We believe he set a perfect example for human beings to imitate and that humans have an obligation to follow his example in all things. Most important of all, we believe that he suffered and died on the cross as a volunteer sacrifice for humanity in order to bring about an atonement through the shedding of his blood. We believe that he was physically resurrected and that he ascended into the heavens, from which he will come at the end of this world to establish his kingdom upon the earth and eventually to judge both the living and the dead.[3]

Finally, it is to Jesus Christ as Savior and Lord that the Book of Mormon as scripture and that Joseph Smith as a prophet bear witness. The title page of the Book of Mormon states that the book was written "to the convincing of the Jew and Gentile that Jesus is the Christ, the Eternal God, manifesting himself unto all nations." The Prophet Joseph Smith, together with Sidney Rigdon, bore the following witness as recorded in the Doctrine and Covenants:

And now, after the many testimonies which have been given of him, this is the testimony, last of all, which we give of him: That he lives!

For we saw him, even on the right hand of God; and we heard the voice bearing record that he is the Only Begotten of the Father —

That by him, and through him, and of him, the worlds are and were created, and the inhabitants thereof are begotten sons and daughters unto God. (D&C 76:22–24.)

In our own generation, less than two weeks before his death in 1985, Elder Bruce R. McConkie, one of the Twelve Apostles of the LDS church, offered the following testimony of Jesus:

And now, as pertaining to this perfect atonement, wrought by the shedding of the blood of God — I testify that it took place in Gethsemane and at Golgotha, and as pertaining to Jesus Christ, I testify that he is the Son of the Living God and was crucified for the sins of the world. He is our Lord, our God, and our King. This I know of myself independent of any other person.

I am one of his witnesses, and in a coming day I shall feel the nail marks in his hands and in his feet and shall wet his feet with my tears.

But I shall not know any better then than I know now that he is God's Almighty Son, that he is our Savior and Redeemer, and that salvation comes in and through his atoning blood and in no other way.

God grant that all of us may walk in the light as God our Father is in the light so that, according to the promises, the blood of Jesus Christ his Son will cleanse us from all sin.

In the name of the Lord Jesus Christ, amen.[4]

To these scriptural and prophetic witnesses I add my own humble affirmation. Though all the world may say that Latter-day Saints do not know or love or worship Jesus Christ, I know that we do, and if this is not the issue in question, or if this is not enough to be counted a Christian, then the word has lost its meaning.

Notes

Preface

1. See *Deseret News*, 25 July 1986, p. A10.

Chapter 1. The Exclusion by Definition

1. See Wayne A. Meeks, foreword in Robert M. Grant, *Gods and the One God*, vol. 1 of the *Library of Early Christianity* (Philadelphia: Westminster Press, 1986), p. 13.

Chapter 2. The Exclusion by Misrepresentation

1. See, for example, N. Cohn, *The Pursuit of the Millennium* (New York: Oxford University Press, 1961), pp. 76–80 and illus. 4.

2. This is surely one sense in which the Latter-day Saints' eleventh article of faith should be understood—"We claim the privilege of worshiping Almighty God according to the dictates of our own conscience, and allow all men the same privilege, let them worship how, where, or what they may."

3. As reported in *Millennial Star* 42 (15 November 1880): 724; emphasis added.

4. B. H. Roberts, sermon of 10 July 1921, delivered in Salt Lake Tabernacle, printed in *Deseret News*, 23 July 1921, sec. 4, p. 7; emphasis added.

5. Joseph Smith, *History of The Church of Jesus Christ of Latter-day Saints*, ed. B. H. Roberts, 7 vols. (Salt Lake City: The Church of Jesus Christ of Latter-day Saints, 1932–51), 5:265.

6. This is the theme of the Latter-day Saints' eighth article of faith —"We believe the Bible to be the word of God as far as it is translated correctly; we also believe the Book of Mormon to be the word of God."

7. Roberts, in *Deseret News,* 23 July 1921, sec. 4, p. 7.

8. See *Deseret News,* 25 July 1860, pp. 162–63; reprinted in *Deseret News,* 23 August 1865, pp. 372–73.

9. See, for example, D&C 13:1; 27:12–13; 65:2; 81:2; etc., but particularly 107:30–32.

Chapter 3. The Exclusion by Name-Calling

1. The rest of the definitions under this entry refer to nonreligious uses of the term.

2. Walter Martin, *The New Cults* (Ventura, Calif.: Regal Books, 1980), pp. 17–21.

3. Martin, *New Cults,* p. 21; emphasis added.

Chapter 4. The Historical or Traditional Exclusion

1. For example, 1 Timothy 4:1–3 and 2 Timothy 3:1–7 repeat the Pauline warning. Jude 1:17–18 informs us that the other Apostles issued the same warning. And 2 Thessalonians 2:7–11; 1 Timothy 1:15; and 3 John 1:9–10 offer a contemporary witness that the predicted rebellion (apostasy) was taking place already.

2. See, for example, *Table Talk,* no. 4487 (11 April 1539) in T. Tappert and H. Lehmann, eds., *Luther's Works* (Philadelphia: Fortress, 1955), 54:346.

3. The Roman Catholic church recognizes twenty-one ecumenical councils, the last of which was the Second Vatican Council (1962–65).

4. The term *traditional church* is used here according to the Western bias. One could just as easily say, using an Eastern bias, that Roman Catholics and all subsequent Protestant denominations rejected the traditional church after A.D. 1054; or one could even adopt the Armenian, Syrian, and Coptic Orthodox viewpoint and insist that the rest of Christendom broke away from the traditional church in A.D. 451.

[5. *Filioque* is a Latin word meaning "and from the Son." Greek Orthodoxy and the Western church disagreed over whether the Holy Ghost proceeded from the Father alone, or whether he proceeded from the Father "and from the Son" (*filioque*). See the discussion in chapter 7 herein.]

6. "Christian Unity: A Sermon by David Steinmetz," *News and Notes* 5 (April 1990): 6.

7. Roger Williams was the founder of Rhode Island, and George Fox was the founder of the Society of Friends (or Quakers).

8. Kenneth Scott Latourette, *A History of Christianity* (New York: Harper and Row, 1953), p. 818.

9. Francis X. Weiser, *Handbook of Christian Feasts and Customs* (New York: Harcourt, Brace, and Co., 1958), notes the pagan connections of Ember Days (pp. 31–32), processions and litanies (pp. 39–40), the Easter water (pp. 162–63), Saint Stephen's Day (pp. 128–29), Epiphany (pp. 141–42), the feast of Saint Valentine (pp. 318–19), the feast of Saint John the Baptist (pp. 329–31), and the feast of Saint Peter and Saint Paul (p. 333). These examples could be multiplied many times over.

10. Cf. Mason I. Lowance, *Increase Mather* (New York: Twayne, 1974), p. 126.

11. See Weiser, *Handbook*, pp. 60–63. The occasion, of course, is not pagan, but the customs and methods of celebrating the occasion most assuredly are.

12. See M. Leach and J. Fried, *Standard Dictionary of Folklore, Mythology, and Legend* (New York: Harper and Row, 1972), p. 966.

13. See, for example, J. N. D. Kelly, *Early Christian Doctrines*, rev. ed. (New York: Harper, 1978), pp. 3–4: "There is an extraordinary contrast, for example, between the versions of the Church's teaching given by the second-century Apostolic Fathers and by an accomplished fifth-century theologian like Cyril of Alexandria."

14. Maurice Wiles, *The Making of Christian Doctrine* (Cambridge: Cambridge University Press, 1967), p. 28.

15. Edwin Hatch, *The Influence of Greek Ideas and Usages upon the Christian Church* (1890; reprint, Gloucester, Mass.: Peter Smith, 1970), p. 350.

16. Hatch, *Influence of Greek Ideas*, pp. 328–29. For a more recent statement of the same points made by Hatch, see R. P. C. Hanson, "Biblical Exegesis in the Early Church," in *The Cambridge History of the Bible*, ed. P. Ackroyd and C. Evans (Cambridge: Cambridge University Press, 1970), 1:433–34, 449–50.

17. Cp. W. D. Davies, "Israel, the Mormons and the Land," in *Reflections on Mormonism*, ed. Truman G. Madsen (Provo, Utah: Religious Studies Center, Brigham Young University, 1978), pp. 79, 91.

18. The seven traditional sacraments are baptism, confirmation, penance (confession), the Lord's Supper, marriage, holy orders (receiving the priesthood), and the anointing of the sick (known as "extreme unction" until the change of name made by the Second Vatican Council). Though they preserve all seven sacraments, Latter-day Saints don't use the term *sacrament* in the traditional sense.

19. Of course this does not exhaust the meaning of the symbol for Mormons or for other Christians. The "rock" is also Christ (1 Corinthians 10:4; Helaman 5:12) and the principle of revelation (see Joseph Smith, *Teachings of the Prophet Joseph Smith*, sel. Joseph Fielding Smith [Salt Lake City: Deseret Book Co., 1938], p. 274).

20. See, for example, Marjorie Warkentin, *Ordination* (Grand Rapids, Mich.: Eerdmans, 1982), particularly pp. 183, 188.

21. See F. L. Cross and E. A. Livingstone, eds., *The Oxford Dictionary of the Christian Church*, 2d ed. (London: Oxford University Press, 1974), p. 57.

22. See chapter 7, note 1, herein.

Chapter 5. The Canonical or Biblical Exclusion

1. For a scholarly discussion of the dates, see Feine, Behm, and Kümmel, *Introduction to the New Testament* (Nashville: Abingdon, 1966).

2. It is estimated that four of these 362 were at one time complete Bibles, though none of the four (Sinaiticus, A, B, and C) has survived intact.

3. See Bruce M. Metzger, *Manuscripts of the Greek Bible: An Introduction to Greek Paleography* (New York: Oxford University Press, 1981), pp. 54–55.

4. See, for example, R. Spivey and M. Smith, *Anatomy of the New Testament* (New York: Macmillan, 1982), pp. 62–66, or Frederick Gast, "Synoptic Problem," in *The Jerome Biblical Commentary*, ed. Raymond E. Brown, Joseph A. Fitzmyer, and Roland E. Murphy (Englewood Cliffs, N.J.: Prentice-Hall, 1968), 2:1–6, for Protestant and Catholic treatments, respectively.

5. The Greek word *teleios*, translated in 2 Timothy 3:17 as "perfect," more often means "complete," "whole," "ripe," "ready," or "initiated" than it does "unimprovable."

6. See Hennecke, Schneemelcher, and Wilson, eds., *New Testament Apocrypha*, 2 vols. (Philadelphia: Westminster Press, 1963–66), 1:42–45.

7. Eusebius, *History of the Church*, 3.25.1–7.

8. The total comes to twenty-eight because Eusebius listed Revelation as both recognized and spurious, "as it seems right" to the reader.

9. Bruce M. Metzger, *The Canon of the New Testament* (Oxford: Clarendon Press, 1987), p. 209.

10. Quoted in Metzger, *Canon of the New Testament*, p. 313.

11. See Hennecke, Schneemelcher, and Wilson, *New Testament Apocrypha* 1:45–46.

12. See the discussion in Metzger, *Canon of the New Testament*, pp. 218–23.

13. A lectionary is the official list of scriptures appointed and authorized to be read in public worship services.

14. For example, the Church of England made its canon official in *The Thirty-nine Articles* (Article 6) in 1563.

15. See W. G. Kümmel, "The Continuing Significance of Luther's Prefaces to the New Testament," *Concordia Theological Monthly* 37 (1966): 573–81.

16. Metzger, *Canon of the New Testament*, p. 245, but see his entire discussion on pp. 241–46.

17. John Oecolampadius, *Epistolarum libri quattuor* (Basle, 1536).

Chapter 6. The Doctrinal Exclusion

1. President Snow often referred to this couplet as having been revealed to him by inspiration during the Nauvoo period of the Church. See, for example, *Deseret Weekly* 49 (3 November 1894): 610; *Deseret Weekly*

57 (8 October 1898): 513; *Deseret News* 52 (15 June 1901): 177; and Journal History of the Church, 20 July 1901, p. 4.

2. Irenaeus, *Against Heresies*, bk. 5, pref.

3. Irenaeus, *Against Heresies*, 4.38. Cp. 4.11 (2): "But man receives progression and increase towards God. For as God is always the same, so also man, when found in God, shall always progress towards God."

4. Clement of Alexandria, *Exhortation to the Greeks*, 1.

5. Clement of Alexandria, *The Instructor*, 3.1. See also Clement, *Stromateis*, 23.

6. Justin Martyr, *Dialogue with Trypho*, 124.

7. Athanasius, *Against the Arians*, 1.39, 3.34.

8. Athanasius, *De Inc.*, 54.

9. Augustine, *On the Psalms*, 50.2. Augustine insists that such individuals are gods by grace rather than by nature, but they are gods nevertheless.

10. Richard P. McBrien, *Catholicism*, 2 vols. (Minneapolis: Winston Press, 1980), 1:146, 156; emphasis in original.

11. Symeon Lash, "Deification," in *The Westminster Dictionary of Christian Theology*, ed. Alan Richardson and John Bowden (Philadelphia: Westminster Press, 1983), pp. 147–48.

12. For a longer treatment of this subject, see Jules Gross, *La divinisation du chrétien d'après les pères grecs* (Paris: J. Gabalda, 1938).

13. Paul Crouch, "Praise the Lord," Trinity Broadcasting Network, 7 July 1986.

14. Robert Tilton, *God's Laws of Success* (Dallas: Word of Faith, 1983), pp. 170–71.

15. Kenneth Copeland, *The Force of Love* (Fort Worth: Kenneth Copeland, n.d.), tape BCC-56.

16. Kenneth Copeland, *The Power of the Tongue* (Fort Worth: Kenneth Copeland, n.d.), p. 6. I am not arguing that these evangelists are mainline evangelicals (though they would insist that they are), only that they are Protestants with large Christian followings.

17. C. S. Lewis, *The Weight of Glory and Other Addresses*, rev. ed. (New York: Macmillan, Collier Books, 1980), p. 18.

18. C. S. Lewis, *Mere Christianity* (New York: Macmillan, 1952; Collier Books, 1960), p. 153. Cp. p. 164, where Lewis describes Christ as "finally, if all goes well, turning you permanently into a different sort of thing; into a new little Christ, a being which, in its own small way, has the same kind of life as God; which shares in His power, joy, knowledge and eternity." See also C. S. Lewis, *The Screwtape Letters*, rev. ed. (New York: Macmillan, 1982), p. 38, where the tempter Screwtape complains that God intends to fill heaven with "little replicas of Himself."

19. Lewis, *Mere Christianity*, p. 154.

20. Lewis, *Mere Christianity*, pp. 174–75. For a more recent example of the doctrine of deification in modern, non-LDS Christianity, see M. Scott Peck, *The Road Less Traveled* (New York: Simon and Schuster, 1978), pp. 269–70: "For no matter how much we may like to pussyfoot around it, all of us who postulate a loving God and really think about it even-

tually come to a single terrifying idea: God wants us to become Himself (or Herself or Itself). We are growing toward godhood."

21. Most critics are surprised to know how highly the thinking of C. S. Lewis is respected by Latter-day Saint readers.

22. See, for example, John Strugnell, *The Angelic Liturgy at Qumran — 4 Q Serek Sirot 'Olat Hassabat* in *Supplements to Vetus Testamentum* VII [Congress Volume, Oxford 1959], (Leiden: Brill, 1960), pp. 336–38, or A. S. van der Woude, "Melchisedek als himmlische Erlösergestalt in den neugefundenen eschatologischen Midraschim aus Qumran Höhle XI," *Oudtestamentische Studiën* 14 (1965): 354–73.

23. James S. Ackerman, "The Rabbinic Interpretation of Psalm 82 and the Gospel of John," *Harvard Theological Review* 59 (April 1966): 186.

24. J. A. Emerton, "The Interpretation of Psalm 82 in John 10," *Journal of Theological Studies* 11 (April 1960): 329, 332. This was also the view of Saint Augustine in writing of this passage in *On the Psalms,* 50.2: "It is evident, then, that he has called men 'gods,' who are deified by his grace" (cf. also 97.12).

25. Clement of Alexandria, *Stromateis,* 7.10.

Chapter 7. The Doctrinal Exclusion: Trinity and the Nature of God

1. What is erroneously called the Nicene Creed by modern Christians was actually not a product of the Council of Nicaea nor of the Council of Constantinople (A.D. 381) but of the later Council of Chalcedon. See J. N. D. Kelly, *Early Christian Creeds* (London: Longmans, 1960), pp. 296–98.

2. The important trinitarian word *substance* (Greek *ousia*) is never used in scripture in relation to God. The word does appear twice in the New Testament (Luke 15:12, 13) but only to designate the "substance" squandered by the prodigal son.

3. Tertullian, *Against Praxeas,* 3, 11, 12. Theophilus of Antioch used a slightly different term (*trias*) in *Ad Autolycum,* 2.15, written at the end of the second century.

4. See Maurice Wiles, *The Making of Christian Doctrine* (Cambridge: Cambridge University Press, 1967), pp. 19, 24–28.

5. Wiles, *Making of Christian Doctrine,* p. 4.

6. Wiles, *Making of Christian Doctrine,* p. 144.

7. Edmund J. Fortman, *The Triune God: A Historical Study of the Doctrine of the Trinity* (Philadelphia: Westminster Press, 1972), pp. 14, 16, 29.

8. Fortman, *Triune God,* pp. 22–23.

9. Fortman, *Triune God,* pp. 32, 35.

10. In P. Achtemeier, ed., *Harper's Bible Dictionary* (San Francisco: Harper and Row, 1985), p. 1099. This scholarly dictionary was compiled with the help of the Society of Biblical Literature.

11. J. Fitzmyer, *Pauline Theology: A Brief Sketch* (Englewood Cliffs, N.J.: Prentice-Hall, 1967), p. 42.

12. R. L. Richard, "Trinity, Holy," in *New Catholic Encyclopedia*, 15 vols. (New York: McGraw-Hill, 1967), 14:295.

13. Fortman, *Triune God*, p. 44.

14. J. N. D. Kelly, *Early Christian Doctrines*, rev. ed. (New York: Harper, 1978), p. 95.

15. Kelly, *Early Christian Doctrines*, pp. 87–88. According to R. L. Richard, *New Catholic Encyclopedia* 14:299, "the formulation 'one God in three Persons' was not solidly established, certainly not fully assimilated into Christian life and its profession of faith, prior to the end of the 4th century. . . . Among the Apostolic Fathers, there had been nothing even remotely approaching such a mentality or perspective."

16. In F. L. Cross and E. A. Livingstone, eds., *The Oxford Dictionary of the Christian Church*, 2d ed. (London: Oxford University Press, 1974), p. 1394. R. L. Richard refers to writings of Eusebius of Caesarea as "blatantly subordinationist" (*New Catholic Encyclopedia* 14:298).

17. In Cross and Livingstone, *Oxford Dictionary of the Christian Church*, p. 1319.

18. Justin Martyr, *Apology*, 1.22, 23, 32; 13.3; *Dialogue*, 56. Johannes Quasten, *Patrology* (Westminster, Md.: Christian Classics, 1986), 1:209.

19. See William G. Rusch, *The Trinitarian Controversy* (Philadelphia: Fortress, 1980), pp. 5–6.

20. See Rusch, *Trinitarian Controversy*, p. 6, or Bernard Lonergan, *The Way to Nicaea: The Dialectical Development of Trinitarian Theology* (Philadelphia: Westminster Press, 1976), pp. 40–42.

21. See Kelly, *Early Christian Doctrines*, pp. 232–37, and R. L. Richard, *New Catholic Encyclopedia* 14:299.

22. Eusebius, *Demonstratio Evangelica*, 5.1.20; 4.3.7. Also see the discussion in Kelly, *Early Christian Doctrines*, pp. 224–26.

23. Actually the Creed of Chalcedon. See note 1 above.

24. Frank Gavin, *Some Aspects of Contemporary Greek Orthodox Thought* (London: S.P.C.K., 1936), p. 138.

25. Vladimir Lossky, "The Procession of the Holy Spirit in the Orthodox Triadology," *Eastern Churches Quarterly* 7 (1948 suppl.): 45–46.

26. It was the West, after all, that added the *filioque* to the original Nicene Creed. Cf. John 15:26.

27. C. H. Dodd, *The Interpretation of the Fourth Gospel* (Cambridge: Cambridge University Press, 1958), p. 225. See also Raymond E. Brown, *The Gospel According to John (i–xii)*, vol. 29 of the *Anchor Bible* (Garden City, N.Y.: Doubleday, 1966), p. 167.

28. Brown, *Gospel According to John*, p. 172; emphasis in original.

29. Several of the early Christian writers also understood spirits or souls to have corporeal qualities. See, for example, Irenaeus, *Against Heresies*, 34.1, or Tertullian, *De Anima*, 7.

30. Even Augustine was willing to grant that while the essence of the Father must always be invisible, still he "may have represented himself to mortal senses by a corporeal form" (*On the Trinity*, 18.35).

31. Shaye J. D. Cohen, *From the Maccabees to the Mishnah*, vol. 7 of the *Library of Early Christianity* (Philadelphia: Westminster Press, 1987), p. 44.

32. Cohen, *Maccabees to Mishnah*, pp. 86, 87.

33. See Owen Chadwick, *Western Asceticism* (Philadelphia: Westminster Press, 1958), pp. 234–35, citing a reference in John Cassian, *Conferences*, 10.3; also Sozomen, *Church History*, 8.11.

34. See Henry Chadwick, *The Early Church* (Harmondsworth: Penguin, 1967), pp. 185–86.

35. See Augustine, *Our Lord's Sermon on the Mount*, 2.5 (17): " 'Who art in heaven' — that is, in the saints and in the just. For God is not contained in local space.''

36. For an excellent summary of the doctrine of the impassibility of God, including its Greek origins and its tension with Hebrew biblical thought, see Cross and Livingstone, *Oxford Dictionary of the Christian Church*, p. 694.

37. Van A. Harvey, *A Handbook of Theological Terms* (New York: Macmillan, 1964), p. 129; emphasis added. Or see (the Very Reverend) James Malloch, *A Practical Church Dictionary* (New York: Morehouse-Barlow, 1964), p. 244: "This view seems to conflict with God's love for man, Christ's passion, and other doctrines of mercy and sympathy.''

38. Augustine, *Enchiridion*, 33. Cp. also Augustine, *On Patience*, 1: "For if we think of these [emotions] like they are in us, there are none in him. . . . Far be it from us to suppose that the impassible [i.e., incapable of feeling] nature of God is liable to any disturbance.''

39. These words are derived from Latin and Greek, respectively, and mean literally "suffering (Latin *passio*, Greek *pathos*) with another.'' Since, according to the doctrine of impassibility, God can't suffer, he can't have compassion or empathy, at least not in the human sense.

40. Like the idea of a "square circle,'' this proposition is incomprehensible to the human mind, but it allows contradictory conclusions to be asserted simultaneously — that is, Christ is God and suffers, but God does not suffer.

41. Yet for insisting that the Bible *does* mean what it says — that Jesus was God, that Jesus suffered, and therefore that God himself, in his own divine nature, suffered and died for man — Latter-day Saints are labelled heretic non-Christians.

42. The bottom line, of course, is that the divine nature in Christ never suffers or dies. Saint Leo I, *Tome*, 3–4, in Henry Bettenson, *Documents of the Christian Church* (Oxford: Oxford University Press, 1967), pp. 50–51.

43. Chadwick, *The Early Church*, p. 193.

44. Today the doctrine of divine impassibility is under attack by both philosophers of religion (e.g., Berdyaev, Tennant, Hartshorne) and orthodox theologians (e.g., Brunner, Aulen, Niehbuhr, Barth). See Jürgen Moltmann, *The Crucified God* (New York: Harper and Row, 1974), p. 214.

Chapter 8. The Doctrinal Exclusion: Lesser Arguments

1. Though several nineteenth-century Brethren expressed contrary opinions, there is nothing in the authoritative sources of LDS doctrine that justifies such conclusions (see the discussion on what constitutes official LDS doctrine, chapter 2 herein).

2. In the Garden of Eden, where God could have instituted whatever form of marriage he wished without fear of public opinion or of the U.S. federal government, our first parents were apparently monogamous. This fact should give pause to any who would argue for the universal preferability of polygamy.

3. Latter-day Saints believe plural marriage has been forbidden by the Lord since the turn of the century. One need not assume that this makes God "changeable," for there is ample precedent in the Bible for God giving commandments to one people in one circumstance and then rescinding or changing those commandments for other people in different circumstances. For example, compare Leviticus 11 with Acts 10:12–15, Genesis 17:7–14 with Galatians 5:1–6, or Matthew 10:5 with Matthew 28:19.

4. E.g., Genesis 16:4; 25:6; 30:4, 9.

5. See Deuteronomy 21:15–16. Cp. Judges 8:30; 1 Samuel 1:2; 25:43; 2 Samuel 12:8; 1 Kings 11:3; 1 Chronicles 4:5; 2 Chronicles 11:21.

6. See Matthew 5:17–19; 23:1–3; Romans 3:31; 7:12.

7. See, for example, Edward Westermarck, *The History of Human Marriage*, 3 vols. (New York: Allerton, 1922), 3:50, "Considering that monogamy prevailed as the only legitimate form of marriage in Greece and Rome, it cannot be said that Christianity introduced obligatory monogamy into the Western world."

8. Augustine, *Reply to Faustus*, 22.47; see Philip Schaff, ed., *The Nicene and Post-Nicene Fathers*, First Series, (Grand Rapids, Mich.: Eerdmans, 1983), 4:288. Other than his observation that plural marriage was contrary to Roman custom, Augustine's objections to plural marriage were no different than his objections to monogamous marriage—both involved the risk of sensuality.

9. Robert Holst, in *International Review of Missions* 56 (April 1967): 205.

10. H. W. Turner, "Monogamy: A Mark of the Church?" *International Review of Missions* 55 (July 1966): 321.

11. Luther to Joseph Levin Metzsch, 9 December 1526, in Theodore G. Tappert, ed. and trans., *Luther: Letters of Spiritual Counsel*, vol. 18 of the *Library of Christian Classics* (Philadelphia: Westminster Press, 1955), p. 276; emphasis added.

12. See Ernst Enders, ed., *Dr. Martin Luther's Briefwechsel*, 16 vols. (Stuttgart: Verlag der Vereinsbuchhandlung, 1884–1915), 5:441–42.

13. See Enders, *Luther's Briefwechsel* 9:88, and n. 2.

14. See Enders, *Luther's Briefwechsel* 12:319–20 [*WA, Br,* VIII, 638–44]. Cf. Tappert, *Luther: Letters of Spiritual Counsel,* p. 288.

15. Using this marriage as a precedent, Frederick William II of Prussia later took two plural wives with the sanction of the Lutheran *Hofprediger;* see Gerd Heinrich, *Geschichte Preussens: Staat und Dynastie* (Frankfurt am Main: Propyläen Verlag, 1981), p. 257.

16. See the standard scholarly Greek-English lexicon, William F. Arndt and F. Wilbur Gingrich, *A Greek-English Lexicon of the New Testament and Other Early Christian Literature* (Chicago: University of Chicago Press, 1957), pp. 816–17. There is a consensus among scholars that "perfect" is not the right nuance. The Revised Standard Version renders *teleios* here as "mature"; Bo Frid opts for "initiated" (in *New Testament Studies* 31 [1985]: 608).

17. See Arndt and Gingrich, *Greek-English Lexicon,* pp. 531–32. The New International Version renders *musterion* as "secret wisdom."

18. Robin Scroggs, "Paul: *SOPHOS* and *PNEUMATIKOS,*" *New Testament Studies* 14 (1967/68): 54. Whether Scroggs is right or wrong, this is a matter of interpreting phenomenon *within* the Christian tradition, not *extraneous* to it.

19. See Scroggs, "Paul," p. 37: "The distinction Paul makes between his kerygma [public preaching] and his sophia [hidden wisdom] is thus too clear-cut to permit the conclusion that the content of the sophia is the crucified Christ of the kerygma."

20. At least that is the opinion of John Knox and the *New Oxford Annotated Bible* (New York: Oxford University Press, 1973), p. 1407.

21. Gordon Fee, *The First Epistle to the Corinthians* (Grand Rapids, Mich.: Eerdmans, 1989), pp. 763–64.

22. From *The Jerome Biblical Commentary,* ed. Raymond E. Brown, Joseph A. Fitzmyer, and Roland E. Murphy (Englewood Cliffs, N.J.: Prentice-Hall, 1968), 2:273.

23. *Jerome Biblical Commentary* 2:611.

24. Clement was venerated as a saint in Catholicism with a feast day on 4 December until 1751. See *The Book of Saints* of the Benedictine monks, 6th ed. (London: A & C Black, 1989), pp. 128–29.

25. See G. A. Williamson, *Eusebius: The History of the Church* (Harmondsworth: Penguin, 1965), p. 72.

26. As, for example, at *Stromateis,* 5.1, 5.4, etc.

27. Clement, *Stromateis,* 1.1. See Alexander Roberts and James Donaldson, eds., *The Ante-Nicene Fathers* (Grand Rapids, Mich.: Eerdmans, 1975), 2:302.

28. In Morton Smith, *The Secret Gospel* (New York: Harper and Row), a popular version, and in Morton Smith, *Clement of Alexandria and a Secret Gospel of Mark* (Cambridge: Harvard University Press), for scholars.

29. Or "initiated" (Greek *teleioumenon*).

30. A hierophant is one who teaches the secret mysteries to initiates.

31. Like the hierophant, the mystagogue is one who initiates into the mysteries, the secret rites.

32. Note the imagery of the temple.

33. Smith, *The Secret Gospel*, p. 15.

34. Clement's letter to Theodore was provisionally included in a 1980 scholarly edition of his works, O. Stählin and U. Treu, eds., *Clemens Alexandrinus*, GCS 4/1, (Berlin: Akademie-Verlag, 1980), pp. xvii–xviii; cf. viii. Even F. F. Bruce accepts its authenticity in *The 'Secret' Gospel of Mark* (London: Athlone Press, 1974), p. 6.

35. Eusebius, *The Life of Constantine*, 3.43.

36. See F. L. Cross, *St. Cyril of Jerusalem's Lectures on the Christian Sacraments* (London: S.P.C.K., 1951), pp. 53–67.

37. Cyril, *Procatechesis*, 12. The translation is that of W. Telfer, *Cyril of Jerusalem and Nemesius of Emesa* (London: Library of Christian Classics, 1955).

38. Cyril, *Mystagogical Lectures*, 1.2. Greek *apotasso* can also be translated "to dismiss," "to separate," or "to part." See Gerhard Kittel, *Theological Dictionary of the New Testament*, trans. and ed. Geoffrey W. Bromiley, 10 vols. (Grand Rapids, Mich.: Eerdmans, 1964–76), 8:33.

39. Cyril, *Procatechesis*, 14.

40. Cyril, *Mystagogical Lectures*, 2.3, 3.4.

41. Cyril, *Mystagogical Lectures*, 3.7.

42. Cyril, *Mystagogical Lectures*, 3.8.

43. Cyril, *Mystagogical Lectures*, 3.1.

44. Cyril, *Mystagogical Lectures*, 1.11, 2.1.

45. For the comparative parallels, see Hugh M. Riley, *Christian Initiation* (Washington, D.C.: Catholic University of America Press, 1974).

46. Basil, *On the Holy Spirit*, 27 (66); see Philip Schaff and Henry Wace, eds., *A Select Library of Nicene and Post-Nicene Fathers of the Christian Church*, Second Series, 14 vols. (1952–57; reprint, Grand Rapids, Mich.: Eerdmans, 1983), 8:40–42.

47. See Cross, *St. Cyril of Jerusalem's Lectures*, p. xxii. Any who are still skeptical that a secret ritual, which included baptisms, anointings, robings, etc., was ever a part of Christian orthodoxy should consult Riley, *Christian Initiation*, which describes the practices in detail.

48. In F. L. Cross and E. A. Livingstone, eds., *The Oxford Dictionary of the Christian Church*, 2d ed. (London: Oxford University Press, 1974), p. 1292.

49. The reference is to Moses 4:1 (emphasis added), where Satan's words, spoken in the premortal life, remind us that wanting the credit for what God does was a primal sin, a satanic impulse.

50. Of course, Latter-day Saints also accept as doctrine the biblical passages that teach salvation by grace and justification by faith, but I am interested here in illustrating these doctrines from exclusively LDS sources.

51. LDS commentators are agreed that the word *after* in this passage is used as a preposition of separation rather than of time. The sense is that apart from all we can do, it is ultimately by the grace of Christ that we are saved. This meaning is apparent from the fact that none of us actually does *all* he can do.

Chapter 9. Conclusions

1. This necessarily assumes the intellectual honesty of the critics. The exceptions, of course, are those who employ the exclusion by misrepresentation—and their numbers are not small.

2. The only exceptions are those Sundays when stake or general conferences are held.

3. In fact, if allowed to define the phrase "holy catholic church" nondenominationally, as Protestants do, there is no doctrinal reason why Latter-day Saints could not affirm the traditional Apostles' Creed, of which the preceding propositions in the text are a paraphrase.

4. Bruce R. McConkie, "The Purifying Power of Gethsemane," *Ensign* 15 (May 1985): 11.

Index